Becoming *an* Elephant

Becoming an Elephant: Be a Millionaire with Only 4 Rental Properties

This book is set in the typeface *Athelas* designed by Veronika Burian and Jose Scaglione.

Paperback ISBN: 978-1-967262-41-0
Hardcover ISBN: 978-1-967262-42-7

A Publication of *Rental Property U Publishing*
www.rentalpropertyu.com

| 1 25 25 20 16 02 |

Published in the United States of America

Becoming *an* Elephant

Be a Millionaire with
Only 4 Rental Properties

Heather Lynn Anderson

RENTAL PROPERTY U

Thank you to the many mentors that shaped my life.
And to Aunt Karen, my first mentor.

Table of Contents

CHAPTER ONE

Introduction

It was 1995. I had just turned 16 and it was another sweltering Dallas, Texas summer. My mom, an elementary school teacher, was off for the summer which meant extra chores for me, my brother and sister—it was deep cleaning time. I dusted and vacuumed, while my brother was stationed on the exterior doing yard work and my sister was tasked with organizing her toys. I was not a fan of the tasks and had to be bribed with an allowance every week. On one occasion while dusting glass shelves and souvenirs, I asked my mom a question I had been pondering.

"How much is a million dollars?" I said.

"It's a lot of money," she said.

"Well...how much?" I articulated.

"Just a lot of money." she repeated.

She was a math teacher, after all, and I figured she could frame up an idea of how much a million is and what kind of buying power it held. I probed some more on the topic and she retorted, "A million dollars is too much money, Heather"

Because I was the qualifying type, I pressed on with another qualifying question. It's possible I wasn't clear, I thought.

"Could I ever make a million dollars, Mom?"

"No," she replied, "you won't ever make a million dollars, Heather."

I paused to compute this. By this time I had begun getting paychecks from my first job at the daycare.

"So even if I save every penny I ever make, I still won't have a million dollars?" I enquired.

"No."

"What if I work two jobs and save every penny...will I have it then?"

"No."

"OK...what about three jobs?"

Still, without hesitation, and without considering the possibility, she said, "No, Heather, you will never have a million dollars. It's not possible."

That statement burned within me and etched itself deeply into my spirit. So memorable that I still remember reaching for the high glass shelf and seeing the specs of dust falling in the filtered sunlight, and how tan I was that summer. That was a moment for me. A big moment, actually. I know you have some of those too. Those deep core memories that have shaped your path. Those *moments*. The ones that make up your life reel.

How could my mom be right? Having a million dollars meant you were successful. It meant you got out of being poor or middle class and had a financially stable life. It meant you broke the cycle of the life you came from, which is what most *becoming* stories really are. To me a million dollars was the cost of the ticket out of the life I grew up in. I couldn't accept that this was as good as it could be for me. I wouldn't. And I didn't. I subconsciously made an agreement with myself at that moment.

After all, this was the United States of America and if I worked hard enough without giving up, anything was possible in this land of opportunity for normal people like me. That insight at age 16 has not left me to this day. It had a pull on me for my entire adult life. Yet for the decade to follow I did not quite have the 'how' piece of my millionaire puzzle. I knew *where* I wanted to go and *why* I wanted to go, but didn't know *how* to get there. That is until I learned about **Rental Property Investing (RPI)**[1]. I had seen people make money, but I hadn't seen anyone keep money very well. I was determined to be someone who kept money and made something valuable out of it. That is called *investing*. Making money from your money.

My path was not a straight one, but whose is? I was a normal person after all. I can't imagine that anyone on planet earth, past or present, who is a first generation wealth builder hasn't had some really hard times reaching their goals. You have to figure out how to live the life you want while you are living the one you have. The people who 'make it' to their goal all have one thing in common, they don't give up.

And...I never did.

I met my goal when I was gearing up to buy my 10th real estate asset at the age of 38 on November 26, 2017. I was making a *Personal Financial Statement (PFS)* for the lender and realized I had arrived at my teenage dream. I was a millionaire. However, the celebration didn't go as planned. There was not a parade in the street, awards ceremony or a cupcake bouquet delivered. It was a late, cold winter night, my hair was air drying from the shower and I was sitting in mid-week-wrinkled-pajamas. My assets were full, but my life was so very empty.

My life passed before my eyes in an Ebenezer Scrooge montage sort of way and I became the most depressed I had been in my entire life. I realized what I had given up in the pursuit of that 16-year-old moment that drove my entire adulthood. The biggest achievement of my life felt

1. You will see the acronym RPI used often in this book. It will interchangeably mean Rental Property Investing or Rental Property Investor.

lonely, because I had no one to share it with. No family of my own to celebrate with and reminisce about the journey we took to reach this incredible milestone. It was literally the rock-bottom moment of my life.

WHY AM I QUALIFIED?

Isn't it funny that to be a *Subject Matter Expert (SME)*, there was a point when you did not know anything about the subject at all? You literally knew nothing about the very thing you now understand the most and get paid for. This universal know-nothing phase is called 'the beginning'—and we all have one. But what was it that made the beginning not the beginning anymore? Was it a curiosity that spurred you to action? A gut instinct that led you to learning? Or was it a role model? A family member, mentor, magazine article, quote...or something else entirely? Did it begin at age 6, 15, 23, 34, 46, 55, or 68? Was it a good experience, or a negative one? What was your ignition point? Why are you reading this book?

Most people don't live in miracles; they live in *moments* that build up to what appears to be a miracle. Having a seven-figure net worth is generally not the result of a miraculous one-time deal, but is rather the result of years of sound decisions, discipline and wise investing. I didn't know anything about money when I started making it, saving it and investing it. I do have a finance degree, but let me tell you, finance is much different than accounting and I was never good at being accountable with money (AKA saving and investing) until I forced myself to be. I couldn't bear not having anything of real value to show for my hours worked. I had a big goal to meet. I could see the big picture and knew I had to take incremental steps to get there. That is the only way I knew that normal people could become successful. It was going to take some time. Not a lifetime, but some time.

I had always heard that to be successful, it's about who you know. Well, I was a normal person and normal people don't really know many successful people. The only successful people I knew were my Aunt Karen and Uncle Freddy, but even then I could only watch them from a distance at Christmas and Easter dinners. You will read about their pathway in the last section of the book, the Elephant section.

I could not accept that success was predicated on something you had no control over like who you knew. Somewhere in the world's history of family trees, there had to be a case where someone became successful without knowing people. In other words, someone had to start it. Not everyone is royalty, the child of a celebrity, or has a trust fund, so someone essentially had to be the first. If they were the first in their family to build generational wealth, then they likely 'didn't know anyone of influence.' They just had to declare their will, work hard, take action and adopt the law of *never* giving up. Living in America I knew I had the truth of the *American Dream* to back me up. America the Beautiful would play her role and I would play mine. An agreement was made. So, America and I went into business together. After graduating college in Tennessee, I moved to London UK on New Years Eve of 2002 and then back home to Dallas in July 2003. I started my real estate career in new home sales in a suburb called Frisco, TX outside of Dallas/Fort Worth (DFW), TX in October 2003. I moved back home to take my dad to cancer radiation treatments every day. After he started to feel better, we started to go on field trips after his treatments. One of the field trips was to the Frisco new home sales community because he had a wild hair to buy a rental property...but no plan or approval from my mom, the money manager as she calls herself. He ended up going under contract for two rental properties, but later cancelled them and lost his earnest money of $4,000 because my mom did not agree. She never let him live that down, poor guy. But like many of our stories of *becoming* go, we pick up where our parents leave off. So in a way, I completed what my dad started. Thanks Dad.

Around this time, I began to envision a 30-year real estate career. I broke it down into decades as a *10-10-10 plan*. The first 10-years I would work my butt off, learn everything I could, and go wide rather than deep with my offerings. Say *yes* to anything and everything real estate, and start saving, investing and meeting the people that I am supposed to know. The second decade was to automate what I learned and let the knowledge I built start working for me. That is when I started building and growing companies more strategically with systems and processes, learning about tax structure and asset layering and started to rid myself of what wasn't serving me or my specialty of helping RPIs. I said *no* a lot more and deconstructed things that I didn't want to scale. I started going deep instead of wide in my offerings and knowledge base.

The third decade, which began in October of 2023, was called the mailbox money phase. That was the time frame when investments from my rental property portfolio and the companies I had built started to pay off, I could transition more out of the things I did not want to do and do more of the things I did want to do, such as teaching and training the next generation of RPIs like you. So I hired a couple of business coaches, built and recorded an RPI 101 e-course, started writing this book and built Rental Property U. I want to help people like you get focused so you can take action when you are *Willing & Able*. Real Estate Investing as a whole let alone RPI is often a fragmented space with lots of misinformation, get rich quick schemes, fear, lack of structure, lack of proper expectation setting and accountability. I hope to help change that.

In the last 23 years of my career, I logged 20,000 hours in real estate as a new homes sales person, realtor, property manager, leasing agent, real estate broker and RPI. This is the only industry I have ever been in after university. I have built from scratch and run two operational residential real estate brokerages, co-purchased two small apartment buildings, closed well over 1000 real estate transactions, built my own rental property portfolio, and helped 100's of other RPIs do the same. I have several degrees from the school of hard knocks, most of my training was taken from Trial & Error University and drinking from a firehose was a common strategy I used in the *becoming*. I do not advise this pathway. Burnout, stress, anxiety, workaholism, and very little enjoyment was the result of no systems and processes, lack of planning, expectations not being set properly and not working in alignment with a clear mission for my life personally and professionally. I have a deep desire to help raise you, my RPI children, in a more joyful, peaceful manner. After all, every good parent wants their children to have it better than they did. This is redemption and this is my deep desire for you as well. I will be redeemed knowing my story can help you create your own on a better path than the one I traveled. Just know by reading this one book, you have already learned more than I knew when I was in your shoes. Don't give up your life in the pursuit of wealth. Enjoy the pursuit and take others with you on it. It's much richer that way, dear friend.

When I finally began to read books, almost 10 years into my career and on my way to *becoming*, I was reading books by successful billionaires, but I could not really relate. I always wanted to meet local business leaders, find the case studies and books by the low-key-behind-the-scenes-millionaires that I wanted to be like. Intuitively I knew I probably wouldn't be a billionaire, nor did I really need to be. I knew a few million would work just fine for the *Millionaire Next Door* life I wanted to live.

I figured there are a lot of people like me who desired to be a millionaire vs a billionaire.

This was the community I was looking for as I was *becoming*.

And this is the community I will be talking with in this book.

CHAPTER TWO

The Goal Of This Book

The goal of this book is for your Net Worth of Rental Property Assets to be $1 million or more, aka: For you to Be an Elephant.

Net Worth = Assets (Property Value) - Liabilities (Mortgages)

When you see *grey boxes* like this throughout your guidebook, consider them as lessons, or references. They stand out so you can easily flip back through the book to find the lesson you might want to review.

HOW MANY PROPERTIES DO I NEED TO BECOME AN ELEPHANT?

You can become a millionaire with 4 rental properties. In some markets, you might need 3. In other markets you might need 5. In the introduction section I am going to introduce a plan called the *4-in-10* to help you build a simple formula for *becoming*. The *4-in-10* is acquiring 4 properties in 10 years. You speed it up, slow it down, buy more or less. There are many ways to become a RPI millionaire, the *4-in-10* is only *one* way. Many of the pathways (which are real RPI case studies) I write about did not use the *4-in-10*, because they developed their own method. But, what I have found in my experience is that it is very easy for people to get lost when they don't have a framework of a plan and because this business is long, it is best to have a plan so you know where you are going.

HOW LONG WILL IT TAKE FOR ME TO BECOME AN ELEPHANT?

I am going to tell you the hard, honest, truth of first generation wealth building for most normal people like you and me. It's probably going to be a couple of decades. 10 years for *acquisitions* and 10 years for mortgage pay off using the *debt snowball method*. Instead of using the money you save for down payments during the initial 1-10 acquisitions, you will use it along with cash flow profits in years 11-20, to pay off mortgages. You are sort of building your own annuity...and that is going to take a minute...

Are you surprised to hear of this time frame? I ask because a lot of people just don't want to hear the reality that building first generation wealth takes this kind of time. Time is indeed the secret sauce. Are you going to slap me if I tell you it's not a bad thing? Some sources report that 70% of lottery winners go on to declare bankruptcy. Why? Well for those of us who have become first generation millionaires the old fashioned way of earning and investing, you learn a lot of things about money along the way. Money lesson #1 is how to make it. Important lesson #2 is how to keep it. There is a magic that happens when you use your time and labor to build money over the variable of time. That hard-earned-money-built-over-time type of money has a different value. I am not saying lottery winners don't value their jackpot, but that is a *get rich quickly* type of wealth. It is very different from a *get rich slowly* type of wealth I can assure you. So if you are agreeing to be a first generation millionaire, your migration will be more rich along the way if you decide to enjoy it. **You have a 99% chance of getting rich slowly and a 1% chance of getting rich quickly.** Every Elephant pathway in this book played the odds, and it worked. And every single one of their stories of *becoming* took the time I am speaking about. You will see when you start reading them.

I believe that at the end of your one wild and precious life your story will be of a great migration of *Becoming an Elephant*. After all, if you don't have any other generational wealth building plans at the moment, consider adopting the *4-in-10* or whatever pathway you choose and *execute* (which means to get started) because no matter what investment vertical you choose to do, the secret to getting ahead is getting started.

If you look around at most normal people in your sphere of influence that are 20 years older than you, you likely won't find many of them to be millionaires. Why? Because, they probably thought 20 years was way too long, 20 years ago. Almost all of them could have been millionaires by now if they gave their dollars clear jobs along the way. Every dollar needs a job. Investments are jobs for your dollars. And RPI acts as sort of a savings and investment jail because this investment is illiquid and has a long term appreciation plan inherently attached to it. That can be a very good thing for those of us who are learning money lesson #1 (earning) and #2 (keeping) in tandem. You have to find a way to invest for your future self. That is if you truly want to get ahead financially. Not everyone does. And there is no shame in that, but let's be honest, most people do.

You now have a plan. A formula. You can adjust this formula as you go, that is called a *pivot*. It simply means to change directions. And all investors do it. You almost have to in order to survive the hard times and thrive in the good.

You will learn about many other RPI pathways in this book. You will read stories about clients and contacts of mine who *became* and those who got lost along the way. Many Elephant's had a very strong *willingness* and very strong *ability*. Many of them didn't have a clear plan, like you will when you begin, but they are really the exception to the rule. Most normal people like you and me need a plan. You will see how our Top Fox Ben was able to thrive once he got one. Without a plan, pathway and the right leadership...and because the great migration is long, Elephants-to-be simply get lost. *Becoming an Elephant* isn't hard, it's long. And long turns into hard when you don't have a strong willingness and ability, plan and community.

Below is a visual of how the 4-in-10 looks.

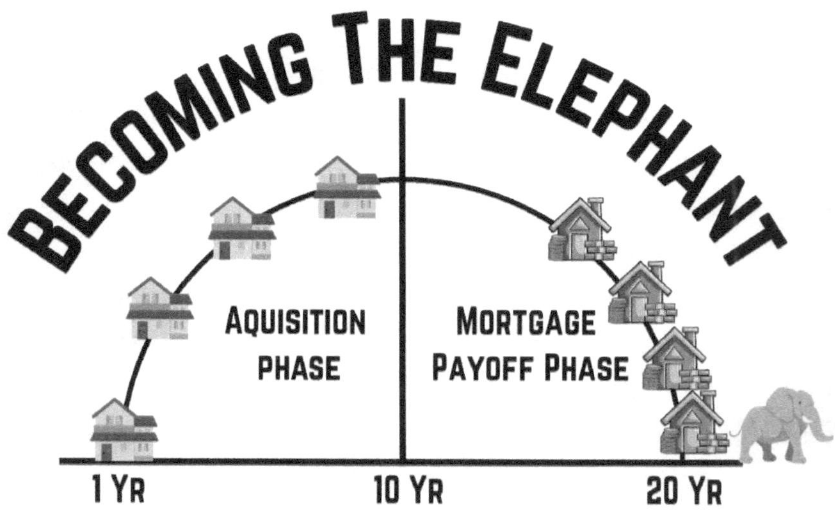

I wrote this as a guidebook. A reference book. Click on the QR code below before, during or after reading this guidebook. The QR code will direct you to our website and can be a compass whenever you need it. If you get stuck, want to grow, pivot, want to review your pathway, or learn more, then click the QR code and see what we are up to in the RPI world.

If you don't think one million is enough, then let's start with this incredible financial goal and grow from there. It is still pretty rare to be a millionaire in the world and in America....(and please note that you have the highest chance of being a millionaire in America). That is exactly why the *American Dream* is still alive and well.

More than 680,000 new people became millionaires in 2024, according to the latest annual report by Swiss bank UBS. In terms of percentage growth, the greatest increase was in Turkey, which saw an 8 percent rise in the number of millionaires year-on-year, followed by the United Arab Emirates, which saw an increase of 5.8 percent. Over the next five years, UBS analysts forecast North America and Greater China to be the main drivers of global wealth growth.

As the following chart shows, the number of U.S. dollar millionaires has risen sharply since the beginning of the 21st century. In 2000, there were 14.7 million millionaires in the analyzed countries. In 2024, there were almost 60 million - a fourfold increase in twenty years (~300 percent). If we compare this figure with the fight against extreme poverty, the number of people below the global poverty line - which today stands at $3.00 a day - has declined at a much slower rate. At the turn of the century, there were 1.7 billion people living in extreme poverty, compared with around 808 million today, a drop of around 52 percent.

The United States is by far home to the largest contingent of dollar millionaires: 23.8 million in 2024, representing 7 percent of the country's population. Next on this list is China with 6.3 million (0.4 percent of the population), while France completes the podium with

2.9 million (4.2 percent of the population). China has seen millionaire numbers rise especially fast since 2000.

Millionaire numbers are projected to increase until 2028 in the vast majority of the 56 countries in UBS's sample. Two exceptions are the Netherlands and the United Kingdom. In the latter country, there will be a projected 3.1 percent - or around 81,500 - fewer millionaires in 2028 than in 2024.

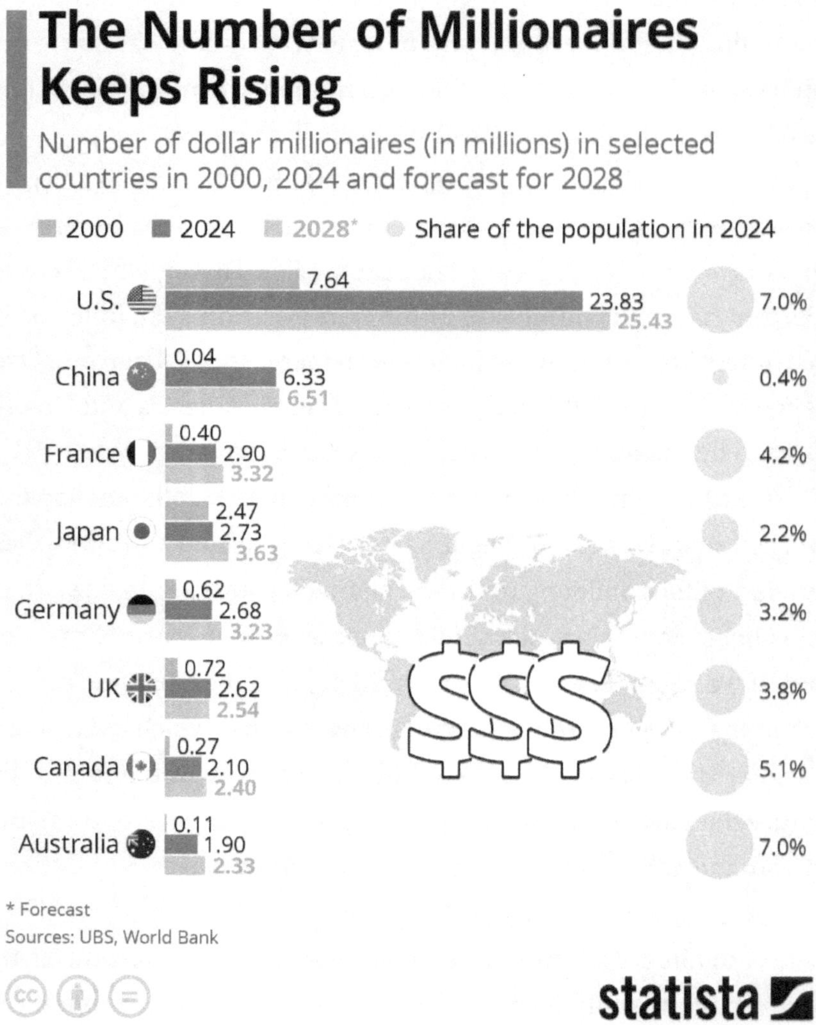

So we are going to focus on getting you into the 7% club. Deal? You can either stay there or grow from there. Becoming a millionaire with the *4-in-10* or whatever pathway you choose is *how* we are going to do it.

The *4-in-10* will have you acquiring a property every 2.5 years on average. You don't like that? Don't forget to exert your free will and *pivot* your pathway, which is why I wrote about so many other RPI pathways for you to choose from in the pages to follow as well as some investors that are still *becoming* as well as some that started out but got lost along the way. You don't need to decide on the *4-in-10* pathway right now because you are to read all the RPI pathways in this book (we will use the term pathway interchangeably with case study in this book) so you can *Pick Your Pathway* and get started. The *4-in-10* is just one possible pathway you can choose to *execute*. And remember if you end up choosing this pathway you can always *pivot* and go to another pathway as you grow your portfolio. The cool thing about being a RPI is that you have choices. Having choices is what makes life awesome.

Please don't get caught up on the 20ish-year time estimate..I know that makes people want to shut down sometimes...actually most times. I know because I have seen them do so in my presence when I tell them face-to-face. I am aware that we live in a microwave world. There are ways to *Become an Elephant* quicker. I did it in 11-years of RPI, my sister migrated in 15. Many other investor pathways you will read about did it in less than 20-years as well. BUT, I am a huge fan of setting realistic, over-promising expectations because what I have found is that if my investor clients agree to the worst case scenario, then they are never disappointed. However, they are always disappointed if they agree to the best case scenario and it does not materialize as suggested. Very rarely does a best case scenario play out as hoped for, wouldn't you agree? That is just wisdom isn't it? Accepting that many times in long migrations, things go unexpectedly and wise people prepare for these inevitable situations on the front end to best prepare for their journey.

Before we can even discuss this *becoming* proposal, you must first read this book. That is your first goal and it won't take you anywhere near that long...well that is as long as you make an agreement to do so, make a plan and then *execute*. If you have not developed a process for reading a book for personal & professional development, as I didn't for years, which led me to start books and not finish them, here is a simple process you can use.

BOOK READING PROCESS:

COMMIT TO ONE CHAPTER-A-DAY: This book has __ chapters. So that would be __ days to finish.

TIME NEEDED PER CHAPTER: Most non-fiction book chapters, in my experience, are 15-30 min depending on your reading speed, comprehension and ability to focus. Sometimes I have to reread a paragraph or section 2-3 times because my mind keeps wandering.

HOW TO FOCUS: If I can't focus, I will sometimes read it aloud to myself. I will also put on my Bose headphones without any music, just to cut the ambient noise around me, which helps me to focus. Or I will play *Unchained Melody- Orchestra Version* by Maurice Jarre on repeat. I have probably listened to that song 1000s of times for various projects I am either working on (like writing this book) or reading. You have made it this far in life, so I have no doubt that you can focus 20-30 minutes a day for a few weeks to meet this goal.

YOUR FIRST MILESTONE: Finish this book. If you do nothing else with the information in this book, decide you don't want to be an RPI at all or don't start for years to come, please walk away knowing you were a victor. Please make that agreement with yourself now and you don't have to explain that victory or share it with anyone. It's for you.

CHAPTER THREE

The Format Of This Book

The lessons I remember most from my university business classes were case studies. Show me it's possible with someone else and show me how they did it and I can follow in their footsteps. Plus they are stories, and I just feel stories are more relatable and memorable ways of teaching and learning for us all. In whatever topic I am researching, I always gravitate toward case studies. YouTube is a visual case study university, which is why I love it so much. I wanted to share the story of those who worked the 9-5 job, drove the old 200,000 mile car, lived in the suburbs in their early 20s when all their friends were living in the city, worked several jobs, had the kids, paid for their college tuition, saved money in a spending culture, and got ahead in a way that less than 10% of Americans have...by becoming first generation millionaires. Believe me friend, it's attainable for you. I will show you how to get rich slowly by sharing these RPI pathways (cash studies) of other normal people like you and me who did it with only a few rental properties. I want to make it as clear as I can that I am not trying to sell you something or convince you to do x or y. I want to give an honest accounting of these RPI pathways so you can decide what it is you want to do with your one wild and precious life. In these RPI pathways, I am going to show you some real returns and portfolio numbers. I call this their *Rental Property Quilt (RPQ).* Some of these *RPQ* will be more in-depth than others. Some of the Elephant's *RPQ* won't be in the print of the book at all because their portfolios are too detailed to fit in the type setting. Therefore, many of those you can find by clicking the *QR code.* Also not every *RPQ* will have the same format. Don't get too caught up in the *RPQs.* They are just there as a general offering of the returns you can make. You will notice a key element in all of them. Their values always go up, it's just a function of time.

To choose the case study pathways for this book, I analyzed 100 of my personal and most memorable RPI clients and contacts. Of those, I boiled them down into personality categories based on some patterns I noticed. There ended up being four groups.

I named each group after an animal so I could better explain their investor pathways and try to help us both have fun while doing it. In your *Becoming an Elephant* guidebook, you will meet three other animals that you could get stuck in, thus losing your way to *Becoming an Elephant.* You will read about several different pathways within these animal groups so you can be aware that there are many risks on your Elephant migration.

THE 4 RPI ANIMALS:

Fox- Someone who values others, follows the advice of their experienced real estate team, is coachable, knows how to delegate, and has a mutual-fund mind when it comes to real estate investing vs a day trader mindset and doesn't step over dollars to pick up pennies. They understand the secret to getting ahead is getting started. They are usually well researched and just need the right person to help them execute their plan. They are also willing to pivot when their leader advises them to do so. They are very goal oriented and realistic. However, since they are so competent and capable, they can get caught up on another investing vertical, thus abandoning their RPI *becoming* plan.

Lone Wolf- The DIY type. Our investor wolf has a Lone Wolf mindset, not a pack mindset. Often think they know more than the specialists they hire. They are prideful. They are usually the controlling, distrusting, micro-manager type. Most people don't enjoy working with them. Not very loyal. If things go wrong, it's usually everyone else's fault. They research in-depth, but consider the research more valuable than their team's knowledge and experience. They usually don't have a good experience no matter what happens because of their cynical mind. Many times Lone Wolves hit the mark of being a millionaire, but they leave their win-lose signature in the world while doing it.

Goldfish- They have very narrow and specific visions that are not always realistic. They agree to change, but often forget or disregard that agreement. Many of them drop off because it's hard for them and their team to stay motivated looking for a needle in a haystack. Their research is usually word-of-mouth or hearsay, which usually makes their expectations unrealistic. They put the horse before the cart. They are loyal however and appreciate their team. Which means they trust their leader, but don't necessarily believe their leader's advice. Sometimes they hit the goal of *becoming*, but it can take 5-10 times longer than it would if they would play by the rules

Elephant- They are normal people like you and me who built a rental property portfolio that is worth at least $1 million. They got there by valuing the people they hired, leaning on their team's expertise, playing the long game, and staying focused on their *why*. When bad things happened they saw it as a lesson rather than a blame-fest. They are calm, humble, and know things will work out in the end.

They see this as a game, and they enjoy playing it. Many of them want to play it well past the timeline of *becoming*, they want to play this game their whole life. They do it by diversifying the RPI portfolio and deeply desire to be the one who changed the generational wealth in their family downline. They have committed to their mission.

BONUS ANIMAL:

Blue Whale- The Blue Whales are on a whole other level and need their own book to describe their operations, which is why they are not in this book. The Blue Whale is the largest animal living on earth. These are the famous investor names and firms you know because they get a lot of press and are the Mega Millionaires and Billionaires that I read books about early in my own research. They have huge operations, staff, private capital, or they sell stock on the stock exchanges to raise money. Many normal people like you and me look to the Blue Whales as our north star, however, while some will reach Blue Whale status, many won't. Guess what, it's ok. You have other animal pathways to pursue.

You could be a millionaire using any animal personality, but your journey might not be as enjoyable, fulfilling and meaningful. At the end of the day it's how we treat people and experience the joy in life as we live it, isn't it? We can't take any of it with us, after all. Many investors ebb and flow out of each of these animals on their migration. You will hear testimonies from my own migration about these shape-shifting *moments*. If you decide you want to become a Blue Whale, great, but you must earn that first million before you can earn your first billion right? So that is what we will focus solely on in this book.

WHY THE ELEPHANT?

Elephants are the largest land animal on earth. They are our north-star, the self-made millionaires. But Elephants move slowly. They are herbivores and although the Lion is called the King of the Jungle, Elephants are really the king in my opinion, because the Lion can't take down the Elephant. They are some of the longest living mammals on the planet, are very smart, work together in herds and move slowly to get where they are going. But they indeed get where they are going because they have excellent recall, memory and a migration mindset. A migration is essentially a repeated path to get from point A to point B. Their long lifespan is a result of their large size, complex social structures, intelligence, and memory, which are linked to a slower pace of life and a longer period for learning and knowledge being passed between generations.

Here are some other fascinating facts about Elephants[2] so you can adopt your *becoming* identity even deeper:

- Elephants can cover over 100 miles per day - they move slow, but they can go very far.
- They can live to over 80 years old
- They can weigh as much as 13,000 pounds
- They have the longest pregnancy period of any living mammal, typically lasting between 18 - 22 months
- Baby elephants can walk within an hour of birth and weigh 200-250 pounds
- Their trunk is a sensory tool for both smell and touch
- Elephants only eat vegetables and fruits and eat up to 18 hours a day
- Wild African elephants sleep only about two hours per day

According to herd.org.za 'For an elephant, there is nothing quite as important as the love provided and bonds created by their families.

2. Elephant Jungle Sanctuary. "30 Amazing Facts About Elephants That Will Surprise You." Blog, March 10, 2025. Accessed November 18, 2025. https://elephantjunglesanctuary.com/blog/amazing-facts-about-elephants/?__cf_chl_tk=yBMuPlCLCUiKy7s9PFARiABxHvAQpnJ2Mj8bxSmC4pc-1759448874-1.0.1.1-Lgx_2xeVs9UvMr7E.051eNFY7Rv2GOkMxlPSXpol9eA

These phenomenal mammals depend extensively on one another, not only for protection and survival but also for the emotional connections that are crucial for any elephant to thrive." Additionally, Elephants travel in close-knit herds for safety and social support. The Elephant herd, sometimes called a *memory*, is led by an Elephant Matriarch. These family units, led by the wise matriarch, offer protection for the young and share a lifetime of knowledge about finding food and water. This deep emotional bond and cooperative foraging are essential for the herd's survival and overall well-being. It would be my honor to be your Elephant Matriarch on your migration.

As you read, pay attention to which animal you are now and how to shift your journey to *Becoming an Elephant*. These are normal people like you and me who were learning as they were doing. Most never read RPI books before they started, as you are doing. Build on that confidence, but remember to *execute* when you are *Willing & Able*. If this isn't your investing vertical, go find what is, and *execute*. If you don't *execute*, it won't matter how many books you have read. Knowledge without action is pretty useless, in my opinion, because the secret to getting ahead is getting started.

WHY RPI?

RPI, to my knowledge, is the only investment in the world where you can build wealth using other people's money (OPM) via a *30-year fixed-rate mortgage*. Rental property can act as a forced savings account. Your money is illiquid and for many of us first-generation-millionaires-in-the-making, that is a good thing. As you grow in your new money habits, it will get easier to have $100k, $200k, $300k sit in your savings or brokerage account without you feeling like it is burning a hole in your pocket. It is a process. All first generation millionaires are learning and doing what they are learning simultaneously, which is why it takes time. Lots of two-steps-forward, one-step-back kind of thing.

RPI is different from other investment verticals like stocks, mutual funds, gold, art, and crypto because you can set up an active, properly structured business to take advantage of its most underutilized (and biggest) advantage: tax strategy. When you establish a business entity like an LLC or Series LLC, which is what most rental property investors do, you gain access to the powerful tax code provisions available to business owners. From there, you can get into trusts, infinite banking, seller financing, multiple LLCs, asset layering and protection techniques, and the Rockefeller Method of building and protecting generational wealth.

Following through with The First 4 Pillars after you execute on your rental property is vital to the success of your RPI business. Most investors don't follow through — and I think the primary reason is simply that they don't know what they don't know. The secondary reason is that the name "Rental Property Investor" is misleading. The word investor is prominent, but what the person is really embarking on is becoming a rental property investing business owner. RPI is not a passive investment. It is an active business, and the business side is where the keys to the kingdom are.

If I can impart one thing to you, let it be this: the RPI business is the below-the-iceberg opportunity in rental property investing. Don't neglect these foundational pillars and this ideology.

However, since my gut is that most of our readers for this guidebook will be those who have not *executed* yet on rental property #1, I can't go too far down the rabbit hole on this great 8th wonder of the world opportunity. I could honestly write a whole book on the *RPI Business* (don't worry I will log this idea). You will learn a little more about the foundational steps in setting up your *RPI Business* in the *The First 4 Pillars* when you get to Steve the Foxes pathway.

Pretty much every wealthy person I have ever heard about includes the ownership of real estate and the reason is real estate is a time-tested, tangible, relatable, multi-income streamed investment. And most real estate investments just simply pay off in time! There are *4 ways to make money in RPI* that I will detail out for you below.

4 WAYS TO MAKE MONEY IN RPI:

1. **Net Cash Flow** (also known as cash flow and cash-on-cash return) - This is an Annualized Return recorded as income on your tax return and based off your Income Statement. Basically it is the $ you invest (down payment, closing costs, capital contributions) and how much you get back from that each year (rent - expenses) as a %.
2. **Tax Strategy** (the most underutilized, robust and misunderstood opportunity) - This is an Annualized Return recorded as income on your tax return and based off your Income Statement and Depreciation schedule. This amount will be figured out once you, your Tax Attorney or CPA record all of your personal and RPI income and as well as your indirect business expenses and direct expenses from your RPI portfolio. PRO TIP: There is an iceberg opportunity here and trust me, you don't know what you don't know. This is the game you will learn how to play your entire RPI life and even with just a few properties.
3. **Appreciation of Property** - this is the main way you become a Net Worth millionaire because of the Time Value of Money (TVM). This is an unrealized return and is recorded on your Balance Sheet as an *Asset*.
4. **Mortgage Paydown** (if there is a mortgage) - Your mortgage amount will go down as your tenant pays down your principal balance. You will write off the interest, however, annually on your Tax Return via part of your Tax Strategy. This is an unrealized return and is recorded on your Balance Sheet as a Liability.

I use a calculator I built over the years called my *10-Year Rental Property Evaluator Calculator* to analyze potential rental property for investor clients that gives the calculation estimates on the *4 ways to make money in RPI* as one calculation so I can quickly see if a property works for a client or not. Whoever you hire to acquire your rental property will have some way of helping you to analyze your property of interest. Do not let the technicality of these calculations or lack thereof hold you back. I didn't start analyzing rental property in a calculated way until about 2010, 4 years after I started investing myself. And I honestly didn't really even understand those calculations deeper until I started learning about Tax Strategy in 2014 and even more so when I started consistently doing *PFS* semi-annual audits on rental property portfolio valuations in 2015. You will see that many investors in this book are not highly technical with the calculations and numbers. The reason why is because they are normal people like you and me that just have a few properties and play the long game. The long game only has winners. And the secret to getting ahead is getting started, as long as you are *Willing & Able*.

Before we begin with the qualifying section, let's get the #1 burning question I get from most RPIs out of the way:

"IS NOW A GOOD TIME TO BUY?"

The truth is, if you are *Willing & Able* and the numbers work, then now is always the right time to buy because the secret to getting ahead is getting started. The RPI pathways to follow will testify to this and you can discern this question for yourself once you read them and see the numbers. Your willingness and ability to perform and the plan you build to meet your goals is primary and the numbers are secondary because of *TVM*, which means a dollar today is always worth more than a dollar in the future because a dollar today can be invested and compounded.

CHAPTER FOUR

Willing & Able and BANT

When I qualify potential RPI, I always say you are not buying a pizza, you are going to be buying a highly active, expensive, illiquid, long-term, involved commitment. I have helped qualify more people out of RPI than I have helped to pursue it.

The reason is that above understanding calculations, this being what you think you want to do, you will only ever *execute* if you are truly *Willing & Able*. There is no exception to this rule. This is a RPI law. And you won't hear many other *RPI SME's* talk about it. That is because many lead with the property and not the plan. That has been my experience in watching the industry on a macro level as well as being a part of it on a micro level for decades.

WILLING - Willing means you have a very strong *why*.

Are you Willing? You will hear the word *Willing* a lot in this book. It simply means your *why*. What is your *why*? Is your *why* strong enough to propel you when things get hard or go unexpectedly. Is your *why* strong enough to carry you when it isn't fun any more, and feels arduous. Or when the new shiny investing trend pops up? In this business, like any other business, things do get hard. So your *why* has to be strong enough to pull you through *the hard*, which is really just *the long*. People intuitively know that real wealth takes real time to build if you are a first generation wealth builder. Remember, the reason is that you have to learn how to be rich while becoming rich at the same time, and while taking care of all of your other life responsibilities.

MOST COMMON RPI WHYS:

1. Build Generational Wealth
2. Retire Early - I might never want to retire, but I want to ensure I have the choice to retire should I want to
3. Build Supplemental Income - I won't have a pension and don't believe social security will be viable for me to support my lifestyle so I want to build a cash flow income for my future.
4. Own Tangible Investments (vs stock or mutual funds) - I want to diversify and feel RPI is a safe investment
5. RPI Just Makes Sense to Me: I saw someone in my family/friend group/role model do it and I want to do it for myself.

I'm not saying your answer has to match one of these, but I am saying these are the most common motives. Your *why* can change, but does one of these goals stand out to you? If you adopt a goal, agree with it and commit to it...you will achieve it. Remember we are calling generational wealth $1 million and you can do it with only about four rental property assets and around a couple of decades.

As we go through the book, challenge yourself to consider your *why*. Is it strong enough to get you through negative cash flow, large make-ready expenses, property vacancy, boredom or lost focus on the journey, the bad tenants, the bad property managers, the down market, a host of decisions, having lack of community and the struggles of pioneering your own pathway? **Your *why* is truly everything.** Your *why* is your will. Your will is the thing that drives you, no matter what. It's your Frodo Baggins in Lord of the Rings, Forrest Gump pursuing Jenny in Forrest Gump, William Wallace in Braveheart drive. If your will is not strong, this is not going to be a good investment vertical for you. My advice to our potential investors who don't have a strong will or stomach for RPI is to consider investing in stocks or mutual funds or something less involved. **Remember, RPI isn't just an investment, it is a business.** This book is equally about helping you to decide if this is not the right investing vehicle for you, as much as it is helping you to *Pick Your Pathway* and get started if it is. Be honest with yourself. It doesn't mean it won't be a yes for you one day, if that day is not today. You always have the right to change your mind.

My *why* is: ______________________________________

ABLE - Able means you have the financial ability, authority, realistic expectations of needs and desire to execute in a specific time frame.

Are you Able? I spent a lot of my days as a Realtor and Broker qualifying potential buyers, sellers, lenders, agents and investors. Asking a bunch of digging questions and going deep to peel back the layers of the onion to see if the potential client was able. We use a qualifying method called *BANT*. If you aren't yet working with somebody, then you can use the *BANT* strategy below to qualify yourself initially.

BANT

B- Budget - How much money do you have for the down payment and closing costs? How much money will you have left over? Be honest here. How will you replenish your money once you make this investment? At what pace? What was your savings pace and amount in the past? How long have you saved at that pace? What other debts do you have? Do you have any other large debts coming up? How stable is your job and your pay from that job? Are you salaried or commission based? Basically we want to make sure you are not going to spend every dime on the down payment, closing costs and possible capital improvements. We want to plan for a reserve account. A reserve account is an account that will cover at least 3 months of vacancy to start and we will build it from there.

A- Authority - Who are the decision makers? If you are married, is your spouse on board? What roles do each of you have in the decision making process? If you have a business partner, is the LLC formed and have terms been lined out? Is this the first time your business partner has been in a formal agreement like this? Is it your first time to be in an agreement like this? Was it a conversation in passing or something that has been discussed formally? Who will be on the loan? Who will be on the title policy?

N- Needs - What are your initial thoughts on your property *Buy Box Criteria* (to be defined in detail in Ben the Fox's pathway)? Do you want a house, a condo, a duplex? What is the reason for your choice? Is there a certain school district you want? Do you have certain return requirements? If so, why? Do you need a turnkey property? Do you prefer new construction? It's ok if you don't have the answers just yet. You don't have to answer these questions right now. This is usually about flushing out *burning desire needs* so we can help qualify if the potential investor is realistic or not. Basically are they coachable or stuck in a certain need because they are thinking like a home owner vs an investor.

T- Timeline - All successful and SMART goals (we will expand on the acronym SMART goals when we get to our Goldfish chapter) are bound by time. Since most investors don't have a specific time frame, we help them agree to a reasonable one by asking this question: "are you Willing & Able to execute on your rental property within 6-months? If they say, well the baby is due in 2 months, or I'm leaving for a month long trip to China next month, or I am starting a new job next week, we encourage them to wait, because their specific timing is likely not right. Remember, because they are starting a business vs making an investment, their focus needs to be as much on this as it can. Once their timing is right, we then need to put a clear and agreed upon time frame to execute. Would you have ever turned in your homework if there was no due date? Would a wedding ever really happen without a date being set and then a plan around that date being formed?

So many goals and *moments* in life are around time. When do you start the new job? When is the party? When is your birthday? Would we collectively celebrate holidays if they were not time bound every year on our calendars? I doubt it. Time bound goals are everything. That is the very reason I am putting a time bound focus around how you can build your portfolio with the *4-in-10* pathway.

Being qualified as *able* is the other 50% of the equation to successfully *execute*. But remember you need 100% of this vital formula. Potential RPIs will only *execute* if they are both *Willing & Able.* Please accept this truth.

YOUR TEAM

Finding the right people to help you *execute* on your rental property once you *Pick Your Pathway* and then build your *RPI Business* is very important, but this will come in time. Therefore, I am going to show you the easiest first teammate to find and then you will grow from there using their list of connections and partners. If you want to do this on your own, there is a pathway out there for that I am sure, but the reality is for most normal people like you and like me, we need good leadership to help us get started. And all that matters is that you get started because the secret to getting ahead is getting started if you are *Willing & Able*. Usually a Realtor who specializes in RPI is the easiest, least expensive and most viable pathway for normal people like you and like me.

THE RPI SME REALTOR

How do I find the right rental property? Typically the easiest answer to this for new RPI or bottlenecked investors is to work with a licensed real estate agent that specializes in RPI. An easy way to find that is to look for a residential property manager, as many of them are licensed real estate agents that live, eat and breathe this investment vertical. If you don't know of a local residential property management brokerage, try going to *www.NARPM.org (National Association of Residential Property Managers)* and do a search in your area of interest. If there is no one in your area, do a Google or Chat GPT search with words like *property manager* and the zip code of interest and see what that returns. Start calling. Don't be nervous, most property managers specialize in working with RPIs. That means not only do they qualify tenants and manage properties for RPI's who turn into their landlords, they also help investors buy and sell because they are licensed real estate agents. The best property managers might not even advertise or have too many online reviews because they are usually referred by word of mouth. Don't let a lack of online presence mislead you. Both of my real estate brokerages are very much driven by word of mouth referral business.

Typically realtor services are free on the front end since they are compensated with a commission when you close. The commission can be negotiable (how much, who pays it, etc.) and will be discussed with you by the realtor. An experienced *RPI SME* will always have value. So because Agent A has a commission rate of apple and Agent

B has a commission rate of banana, it might not be wise to go with the cheapest rate. Like everything in life, you get what you pay for. Very few professional services work like realtors do, as most professions charge an hourly fee for the time you use, regardless of the outcome. This alone is a big reason that makes working with a realtor easier for many people. Essentially it's a free service until you close, additionally, most realtors work nights and weekends which is helpful to most investors who still work normal business hours. Please be considerate of your realtor's time, and use Golden Rule practices.

RPI SMEs function like your *coach* and help you keep your eye on your goals through a plan and accountability. They help you build a plan, check in on you, follow up, help you get back on track if you get off, and connect you to the right people to help you get to your next milestone and build your *RPI Business*. I can't tell you how much these nudges matter. Accountability partnership is another huge key to meeting your goals.

We have all had positive and negative coaching relationships, and we can learn through our experiences. We often discover that we get what we pay for. Keep a positive attitude and have the attitude of an Elephant that every experience, positive or negative, is an opportunity to learn and grow and move forward towards the end goal.

RPI SME's will not be quick to sell you something that is not a good fit for you, if they qualify you correctly (unlike a sleazy used car salesman). Most *RPI SME's* don't sell anything, ever. They just qualify you and based on your qualification they share with you the reality of the market and help you *execute* if you are *Willing & Able*. They won't necessarily use this language, but they will be using this process. They know that their own long term success comes from referrals through happy, prosperous clients. If you find someone with full time experience in this field, chances are they have done a pretty good job for a fair number of people or it is likely they would not still be in business. Not a guarantee, but a litmus test. Real estate agents are licensed by state agencies and therefore held to a higher standard. Once you are their client, their license requires them to offer a fiduciary duty to you and most of them take it seriously because that is their livelihood. It's not a perfect system, but I believe it weeds out the ones that don't belong. For example, would you agree that if a restaurant stays open for 10 years they are probably doing something right?

Once you find your *RPI SME*, especially if you are a first timer, they will help lead you on what to buy, where to buy it, what the numbers are, and offer suggestions for who else will be on your team. Remember, this is an investment that looks like a house, but isn't your house. You will have to learn to shift your mindset to think of it like a stock or bond, which is what most normal people like you and me otherwise invest in. It is a shift that your friends and family may not understand. You might find that your friends think like consumers, not investors. Consumer thinking focuses on short term gratification. You are an investor and will be learning to think like an investor.

I promise this is not a work with a Realtor PSA, but honestly it is the best way to get off the ground. The initial phone call is always free and the best place for most investors to start. If you don't work with a realtor and you have never done this before, then no one is representing your interest. This RPI world is a wild and expensive one. Returns can be large - but so can losses when mistakes are made. Getting the best expertise working for you helps protect you against expensive mistakes.

How to Qualify RPI SMEs:

- Do they have RPI and/or Property Management and Leasing expertise and experience in the market area of your interest
- Are they themselves a RPI?

- Confirm if their service is free on the front end and if they receive a commission if you successfully close on a property
- They will very likely have the specialized contacts you need to grow your rental property business along the way, ask them about those partnerships.
- If you work with an experienced RPI SME, they will shoot straight with you, qualify you well and not waste too much of your time or theirs. See how your gut feels about this as a trait of theirs after you qualify them.
- Ask them about their processes after closing and if you call them after you close to ask questions and they can be a real partner for you as you build your portfolio.
- Ask for a reference or two of recent RPI clients of theirs.

THE REST OF YOUR TEAM

The rest of your team will come at the right time and you work with a *RPI SME*, they will likely already have most of your team for you, so please don't be anxious! Trust the process and the right team will arrive when it is the right time. However, here is a quick sneak peak at them as you acquire rental property, grow your portfolio and work toward building *The First 4 Pillars* in your *RPI Business.*

VERSION 1 RPI BUSINESS TEAMMATES:

- RPI SME
- Lender
- Title Company
- Property Inspector
- Home Warranty Company
- Leasing Agent & Property Manager (sometimes the same person and sometimes the same person as your realtor)

- Property & Casualty Insurance Provider (initially for property dwelling insurance and eventually for General Liability Insurance and Umbrella Insurance policies)
- Business Entity Attorney
- Tax Attorney or CPA

Here is a quick definitions guide to some of the RPI terms you have already been introduced to.

QUICK INDEX OF RPI TERMS SO FAR:

- **Becoming an Elephant** - An Elephant is a RPI with at least $1 million in RPI portfolio net worth
- **Becoming** - An abbreviation for Becoming an Elephant...a RPI millionaire
- **Moments** - Lessons or life experiences that have shaped you or core memories
- **RPI** - Rental Property Investing or Rental Property Investor
- **PFS** - Personal Financial Statement - A personal Balance Sheet that reveals Net Worth.
- **Net Worth** - Is your Assets (Property Value) minus Liabilities (Mortgages)
- **SME** - Subject Matter Expert
- **The American Dream** - A belief that there is opportunity here and now and it is up to you to find it and take it until you reach your goals
- **Willing** - Willing is your strong why that drives you
- **Able** - You have the BANT qualifiers to be a RPI
- **BANT** - A qualifying method to discern your Budget, Authority, Needs, Timeline
- **Willing & Able** - These two must be present in order for a RPI to execute

- **Execute** - To close, transact, purchase, acquire a rental property
- **Grey Boxes** - Lessons & takeaways highlighted in grey for you to find easily
- **4-in-10** - A process focused method for RPI to acquire 4 rentals in years 1-10 and pay them off using the debt snowball method in years 11-20
- **Acquire** - To buy rental property. Also known as being in the acquisitions phase
- **Debt Snowball Method** - To use down payments you would have used to acquire in addition to cash flow from some of the 4 ways to make money in RPI to pay off the mortgages. Also known as being in the pay off phase
- **Get Rich Slowly** - You have a 99% chance of getting rich slowly and a 1% chance of getting rich quickly
- **QR Code** - Click to see what additional Becoming information we have for you on our website
- **Pathway** - Case Study of a normal RPI like you and like me
- **Pick Your Pathway** - There are so many RPI and real estate investing pathways to choose from. You just need to pick 1 to get started. I use this term to help you get focused on your Version 1 plan so you can get started.
- **RPQ** - Rental Property Quilt - RPI Portfolio details
- **The 4 RPI Animals** - Fox, Lone Wolf, Goldfish, Elephant. Blue Whales will not be written about in this book.
- **OPM** - Other People's Money - Typically a mortgage/loan from the bank/lender
- **30-Year Fixed Rate Mortgage** - Most common residential RPI mortgage type
- **Active & Properly Structured Business** - Extremely important formula to activate your RPI Business
- **LLC** - Limited Liability Company

- **Series LLC** - A Texas Series LLC is a type of LLC that lets you manage multiple rental properties under one LLC, each with its own assets and liabilities
- **RPI Business** - The often neglected underbelly of RPI and the real opportunity
- **Passive Investment** - Investment when you are not managing people
- **Active Investment** - Investment when you are managing people
- **The First 4 Pillars** - The first 4 foundational activities you do to set up your RPI Business after you execute on your rental property. Business Entity Strategy, Tax Strategy, Bookkeeping & Organization, Annual Portfolio Check-Up
- **The 4 Ways to make money in RPI** - Net Cash Flow, Tax Strategy, Appreciation of Property, Mortgage Paydown
- **10-Year Rental Property Evalualuator Calculator** - A proprietary calculator that looks at a 10 year simulated return of a potential rental property calculating The 4 Ways to make money in RPI
- **TVM** - The Time Value of Money - A dollar today is always worth more than a dollar in the future because a dollar today can be invested and compounded
- **RPI SME** - Rental Property Investing Subject Matter Expert. Usually the RPI specialist Realtor or Property Manager/ Leasing Agent who is also the Realtor. You can find these in many markets on www.NARPM.org
- **NARPM** - National Association of Residential Property Managers
- **AAO** - Accept, Adapt & Overcome
- The secret to getting ahead is getting started - **Mark Twain**
- Tell me, what is it you plan to do with your one wild and precious life? - **Mary Oliver**

There will be many more RPI phraseology throughout the rest of the book. All of them will be *italicized*. Some of them will have footnotes. You can look them up as you go or check the QR code to see if we have added a *becoming* terms index to our website.

DISCLAIMER

I am not a financial adviser. This is just one person's experience sharing stories and concepts from real people who built their own version of the *American Dream*. There are many ways to do this, these are just some of the ways. I am recounting my experiences based on my data collection, my memory, my self-taught spreadsheet skills and my true and honest desire to tell you what RPI is for the normal person, so you can *Pick Your Pathway* and get started if you are *Willing & Able*.

If you pick a pathway from this book that ends up not being a fit for you once you put it in practice, it's ok. It's all about *Accepting, Adapting and Overcoming (AAO)*. *Pivoting*, changing directions. And RPIs, entrepreneurs, business owners (which is what you will be) do it all the time. Not because they have ADD and get bored, but because they are playing the long game and realize it's not the right pathway or possibly even the right investment vertical for them. I am *pivoting* right now by *becoming* a first time author. As a first generation wealth builder, you will have to play the long game. The long game has lots of *pivots*. Remember, you never fail until you give up. So don't give up. And if you set your goal to $1 million and you end up with $856,000. Who really cares? I bet that would be about $856,000 more in net worth than you would have had if you didn't have a clear goal of buying 4 rental properties in 10 years or whatever pathway you pick.

In summary, I do not lead a lab of financial real estate investing analysts, I am not a white paper author, nor have I ever appeared on Bloomberg as an RPI expert. But I do know how to become a millionaire with just a few rental properties and that I can teach you. I also changed some names of our RPI pathway patrons as well as some of their personal *RPQ* information for their privacy.

They are all real people that I know and/or have worked with as their *RPI SME* to help them buy RPI and build their *RPI Business*. I tried to be as true as I could with their data, because I didn't want to inflate anything, try to sell you on RPI or pretend the fish was bigger than it really was. If you are good with the soft science practices I used in this book and conventional wisdom, then let's get started on your migration.

CHAPTER FIVE

Top Fox Pathway

Quick Description: The Fox is an A-client, a joyful peaceful investor who is on their way to millionaire status cruise ship style. They like being told what to do and where to go, but they are no pushovers. They trust, but verify, and depend on the people they hire to lead them to success. They play the long game and know it won't be perfect along the way, but know they will hit their target. They are top quality people.

Have you ever had one of those late nights reading, scrolling, watching, or listening? Not just mindless scrolling or bingeing on Netflix, but taking in information on a topic or interest that captures you? You take notes, draft a plan, make poster boards, and memorize mantras.

What's the topic that keeps you up at night and is on your mind as you wake in the morning? For many, this topic is something other than their actual vocation. They secretly love the thought of working as a basketball coach, but find themselves managing a restaurant. Perhaps you wish you were a museum director, but instead became a teacher. Or maybe you read real estate investing forums relentlessly, but you became a software engineer.

I get it.

We often pick our career pathways based on stability and security, which can be wise. The real estate profession is a tough one in which you eat what you kill with little safety net or predictability of a steady income. I haven't had a regular paycheck since my short stinted job at a Hedge Fund after graduating college in 2002 and I understand the risks...but I understand the rewards too. Those who get started in a real estate career will come to terms with both...or they won't make it.

Your interest may have started from an article about Warren Buffet, or perhaps a friend gave you a copy of Robert Kiyosaki's *Rich Dad, Poor Dad.* Maybe you've discovered that nearly every single member of the ultra-wealthy class owns real estate as part of their portfolio. Despite the books and research, you might still be wondering, *Could I be successful? What if I fail?* Yes, for sure those are realistic and ever present concerns. But, I argue, *what if you fly?*

Part of my job as your coach in this book is to help you figure out if you are actually *Willing & Able*. Those two little, but *oh so big* words, are the cornerstone of real estate investing success as we already discussed. Remember, it is always the right time to buy if you are Willing & Able.

We have a saying in our firm, "Ask us how many houses we have not sold?" We often talk people *out* of RPI because of the misalignment of the two big-little words *Willing & Able.* Some are able, but not willing. Others are willing, but not able. And many are unable and unwilling. Even though I've closed well over 1,000 transactions, I've never *sold* anyone anything—I qualify. And if the potential investor qualifies, we help them *Pick Their Pathway* based on their goals. We then help the investor *execute*, delivering on their *mission (the how),* which is powered by their *vision (the why).* This perfectly embodies how we helped our Top Fox Ben. Ben was *Willing & Able.* We were the strategic *RPI SME* to help him *execute.* And *execute,* he did. A few times actually.

BEN

4-in-5 Pathway including 3 Texas rentals, vacation Airbnb, Cash-out refinances, set up The First 4 Pillars

Ben resides in Massachusetts and is a normal guy like you and me. Ben is a Fox. He is actually a top Fox. Foxes do a lot of research. But after they do the research, they do the most important thing...they take action. They *execute.* Foxes value the advice of leaders they have sought out and although they are scrappy and typically frugal, they are not cheap. This means they are willing to invest to get where they want to go in life. They understand they must use their money today to build their future for tomorrow. They understand the idea of becoming *balance sheet rich* and get the concept that in the long run, with great leaders, they will recoup whatever money they spend to get where they want to go. In other words they know the financial law that states when you invest in real estate assets you eventually get your money back. They typically understand the goal is not cash flow in the early years as their 'cash flow' will come from their paycheck when they are still working their regular day job. Cash flow will eventually come from their rental property assets when they stop collecting cashflow from their jobs. By then the tenant will have paid down their mortgage, rent will have increased, and they will now have monthly profit, called *cash flow.* To be a first generation *RPI Business* owner, this is how it works for most normal people like you and me. We have a job that pays us for our monthly expenses. We use the bank's money as a mortgage to fund our rental property business. In the beginning we break even on our monthly income (rent) and expenses (mortgage, property taxes, insurance, repairs, property management fees, etc). Fast forward 15-years. Our mortgage is paid off, almost paid off, or substantially paid off and rent has gone up, so we now have cash flow to supplement or replace our paycheck income.

Remember you are essentially building an annuity and in order for the rental property annuity to pay out monthly, you must first pay in. Foxes understand this and accept it early on.

It was 2017 when we got a call from Ben. He had recently finished reading his 5th book on real estate investing. You could say he was a long-time listener, first time caller. His research journey began when his daughter was born in 2013 and he wondered, *What am I going to do to set up my kid's future?* He began reading blogs on BiggerPockets.com, researching markets, looking on Zillow.com daily and spending time going down the internet rabbit hole of demographic and population movement reports.

Based on this research, he started to focus on the Springtown, MA area (his home town), the big three of Texas (Austin, DFW, Houston), as well as the Raleigh-Durham "research triangle" of South Carolina. After his research, he felt like any of those places would be a good move. However, what was not a good move was what happened to him for four straight years: *analysis paralysis.*

He describes it as the "perfection is the enemy of good" mindset. While he waited and waited and waited for perfection, he wound up with nothing. Although he would be a first generation rental property portfolio builder, he did have a peek into landlording as a child. He grew up in a converted duplex, which housed his own family on one side and a tenant on the other. He emulated this model with his first home and he lives that way today. But he wanted more.

Some of his coworkers were investing in DFW, Texas and he had heard their stories of success. By the encouragement of his take-action wife, who lamented, "Just do it already!" he was finally ready to stop being bound by his perfectionism mindset, and get in the game. He was officially *Willing & Able*, but he just needed to find a qualified real estate team or agent that could help him build and *execute* a plan.

CONSIDERING A MARKET ATTRIBUTES:

- **No State Income Tax** - There are 9 states that have no state income tax: Alaska, Florida, Nevada, New Hampshire, South Dakota, Tennessee, Texas, Washington, and Wyoming. Granted, in some of the states without income tax, there might be a higher property tax rate, but that is figured into the total rent. It could reduce your cash-on-cash return, but there are pros and cons to everything.
- **Landlord Friendly State** - States have property codes that detail laws and regulations for landlords and tenants in each state. There could be additional city ordinances involved that the landlord would need to follow and even HOA guidelines that trickle down the responsibility ladder even further. There are also federal overlay laws that can show up like COVID era eviction freezes and HUD protected classes. Note that even though some states are more landlord friendly, certain cities within that state may not be. That is the job for the RPI SME to help guide.
- **Good Public Schools**- Great public schools are optimal, but these areas can be costly and the numbers just might not work. Poor public schools often indicate much higher risk including higher tenant skips, lower appreciation, less qualified tenants due to lower credit scores and higher collections. So focusing on Good public schools is the Goldie Locks approach of just right. Good public schools are attainable and attract quality tenants and higher demand, which creates low vacancy. Remember vacancy kills cash flow.
- **'Blue Chip Stock' Cities**- This is a metaphor I have used to describe cities like DFW for years to our out-of-state investors. Blue chip stocks offer stable, long-term, slow but steady, low risk returns. They also have diversified economies and

businesses unlike cities who are heavily weighted in only one industry like Houston in oil and Detroit in cars. One way first time investors can hedge their bet against the pits of economic cycles is by looking at cities that are more stable.

- **New Construction-** Buying brand new construction rental property is a real advantage for RPIs with full time jobs and careers and families and who want an easy set up and approach. This is a really easy pathway for new investors and I advise this pathway for entry level and even seasoned investors as much as I can. The reason is that you get a brand new house, up to code, with the most advanced building materials, and under warranty. That means it is typically turnkey and your capital improvements are very low or non-existent. Also, I have found you get a premium on rent for the first few years. Also homeowners insurance is typically low the first few years because everything is brand new.

In his research, Ben realized Massachusetts was not going to be the place he would be able to build his initial rental property portfolio. Turns out, Massachusetts, especially the Boston area where he lived (established in 1630), has had a few 100 years more build out than the DFW area, for example (established in 1841) . In Boston, they have to build up instead of out due to lack of land. Also they renovate older homes into duplexes (like the one he grew up in, as well as the one he lives in now) whereas in DFW we can build out geographically because there is still a lot of land. In other words, your money goes further in newer markets and the barrier to entry is lower.

After the investor identifies their market area, then they need to define their *Buy Box Criteria.* A property *Buy Box Criteria* defines the investor's criteria for what they are *Willing & Able* to buy. For example, Ben really liked the idea of new or newer construction, because he knew what it meant to have expensive and time consuming repairs and updates on older construction like he had on his personal home. We help our investors build out their *Buy Box Criteria* during their *Investor Orientation*. This is the 2-hour session we have with the decision makers virtually, or in-person if they are local, to build out their RPI plan. We *lead with the plan and not the house*. This is a very important component to the process. Successful processes have order. Step 1, build the plan. Step 2, start the search by executing the plan. I can't tell you how many investors have that critical order reversed.

BUY BOX CRITERIA

Here is the typical *Buy Box Criteria* a lot of our first time investors use:

- **Property Type-** Single family home, condo's, duplexes, triplexes, quadplexes, townhomes, small apartment buildings, or commercial real estate are all examples of property types, and no you can't pick them all. The goal is to be specific. I always advise to keep it simple for 101 investors and go with single family homes (SFH) as long as they are available in the market of choice. We prefer brick over siding houses. It's best if the floorplan is open, not choppy. It's preferable that it does not back up to or sit right next to a cemetery, major road, or light transformer and should have no swimming pool or spa. Pools add additional expenses and liability.
- **Size-** For single family homes, look for 3-4 bedrooms, 2-3 bathrooms, 2 car garage with 1500 - 2500 interior square feet. It's best to not be too large or to have too many bedrooms as you outsize the average renter. 3-4 bedrooms is good, 5 is usually too many. 2500 square feet is good, 3500 is generally too much. You will need to have the RPI SME in your market help you define this. The goal here is to define a size that works for the majority of your tenant base.

- **Age-** 20 years or newer, the newer the better. Brand new construction is ideal, but can only be acquired in certain market cycles and not in all market areas.
- **Lot-** Approximately 1/6th of an acre lot. An acre is 43,560 sq ft (I always remembered that from real estate school as 4 women driving down I-35 going 60 miles an hour). You don't want a lot that is too big as the tenant won't take care of it and doesn't usually see it as a benefit like a homeowner would. It's usually overwhelming to them. You don't want something too small because likely they will have a dog and/or children and they need a fenced-in yard with ample room for play. You don't want something too landscaped because tenants typically won't take care of it. A simple cookie cutter lot is what we are typically looking for.
- **Fence-** A 6-foot tall wood privacy fence. If there is no fence, make sure you can add one. If there is a chain link fence, work a wood privacy fence into your budget. A 6-foot spruce wood (which is standard wood) is perfectly fine. Don't forget to stain the wood to add life to the wood if your budget allows.
- **Schools-** Like we already discussed in the market area attributes, schools are important. Schools are the number one characteristic we look at when analyzing property. They are probably the most valuable element for estimating appreciation over the long run. We categorize school districts as Great, Good, Average, Poor. We will not advise our investors to buy in Average or Poor unless they are buying a property in an area that has other appreciation focused attributes, like being closer to major downtown cities. Because good schools will ALWAYS be in demand for renters and buyers (when our investors want to sell), this is what we focus on primarily.

In my opinion, this is your most basic, neutral *Buy Box Criteria* for first time RPIs. To me, it's like taking the mutual fund approach to RPI. If that is how you like to roll in your Vanguard account, then feel free to use this approach. Once an investor like Ben can attach themselves to a *Buy Box Criteria* picking strategy, they can get focused, look at the choices, run the numbers and choose. This strategy truly shapes out the *how* clearly and effectively.

With the area picked, team built, and *Buy Box Criteria* decided upon, Ben flew into town for one day. We built another process for our investors who wanted to come and see the houses and cities personally. Funnily enough, Ben is rare. Many of our investors have never even stepped foot here and we have never met them face to face and we call this *The Siberia Plan.* It is for our investors that want a digital, hand's off approach. After we *BANT* them, get them approved with our lender, do their *Investor Orientation* virtually, they then rely on us to search, scrub and analyze potential rental properties for them. We then go and walk them, record videos and photos of the rental property along with our *10-Year Rental Property Evaluator Calculator* analysis. We upload our analysis to our cloud software for them and they go 'walk the property' and review the calculator and comparable reports. From there they can ask us questions if interested and decide if they want to make an offer. We go to inspections for them, do final walk-throughs and instruct the title company to set up their remote closing. Many of our investors pick this option because its process is focused and we make it easy for them to *execute.* And no these people are not multi-millionaires too busy traveling the globe. They are normal people just like you and just like me who have Fox mentalities and can rely on their team to *execute.*

The other pathway we have is called *Boots on the Ground.* That is either for our local investors who want to do property tours with us and be involved hands-on or they are like Ben who don't live here but want to fly in for a tour or two to actually see the property with their own eyes. Different strokes for different folks. He flew into town and I picked him up from the airport and started our 8 house, 4 city tour. I was his tour guide as we drove, teaching him about highways, history, demographics, school systems, traffic patterns, major work hubs, etc. We stopped for lunch and decided to walk off our food and stroll to the downtown candy shop for a sweet treat before we hit the road for the second half of our tour.

Still in my tour guide mode, I missed my step, twisted my ankle, and took a painful spill right onto the pavement with candy flying out of my mouth. My ankle started swelling quickly and Ben had to take over being the driver for the rest of the day as it was my right foot and I literally couldn't hit the gas and the brake. His first stop was to get me a bag of ice and I sat in the passenger seat for the rest of our tour with my leg elevated. It was embarrassing to say the least. But Ben, the Fox that he is, just adjusted and didn't let this *pivot* shake him one bit. He had a clear and focused mission, I had already earned his trust as an expert...well clearly not in *walking,* but in the finance of RPI and knowledge of the market area. I hobbled through the tour, he made it back to the airport to fly back to Boston that night and I carefully drove back home with a wrapped foot packed in ice.

Back in Boston and confident in his plan, he wanted to place an offer on one of the 8 properties he saw. I wrote up the contract, sent it to him and his wife to sign digitally and presented it to the seller right after my appointment at the orthopedic doctor. He got his offer accepted and I got confirmation that I had a fractured ankle. Ben was officially under contract for his first official rental property. The inspection was easy, the loan was smooth as he went with our preferred lender, Khai, who specializes in working with RPIs and is one himself...another very important component about building your team. With a clear plan and process in place, Ben *executed* and the rest is history.

Foxes play by the leader's rules, which is why they hire them in the first place and because of that, Ben went from reading, analyzing, researching and dreaming for 5 years to executing on three investment properties in DFW, a vacation home in New Hampshire, and remodeling his main home in the Boston area in the five years to follow. How did he do that? Because Ben is a Fox. He knows how to be prepared and then let those he hired lead him into missional success. He knows how to move when it's time to move.

Here are Ben's rental property building details

- He came into town for a *Boots on the Ground* 1 day, 4 city, 8 property tour and closed on his first rental property in Fate, TX in Dec 2017.
- He came into town for a second *Boots on the Ground* 1 day tour but we didn't find one that would work for him on this tour, so he went back home and we showed him virtually using *The Siberia Plan.* He picked one within a few weeks and we closed on his second rental property in Fate, TX in 2018.
- When it was time to buy his 3rd rental in 2019, he went straight into *The Siberia Plan*. One of the agents in my brokerage had a *pocket listing*[3], that she thought might work for him. It would be a *BRRR (Buy, Rehab, Rent, Refinance*[4]*)* strategy. He initially liked the idea of *pivoting* his *Buy Box Criteria*, went under contract, but found himself not sleeping that well. The contract price was attractively low at $170,000, and was in the more established city of Carrollton, TX, but the property was older than and it needed structural foundation work. In order to do the BRRR, he would have to do non-traditional financing called a *Hard Money Loan*[5], initially. He questioned if he really had the time and risk tol-

---

3. This phrase means an off-market deal, not listed on the MLS.
4. Check out the details about this strategy coined by BiggerPockets.com in resources.
5. Typically a short term, private loan with a high interest rate. A common loan type used by rehabbers or flippers.

erance to veer off to a new business model like this would be. Following his internal peace, he backed out. We returned back to his original *Buy Box Criteria* as property 1 and 2 but changed cities to add a layer of diversification and he felt instant relief. We closed on his third property, using his same *Buy Box Criteria*, in Mckinney, TX in 2019.

- Next he bought a family vacation home in the summer of 2020. It's a peaceful property on the lake near the mountains where people ski in the winter and hike in the summer located in Silver Lake, New Hampshire. Notice the time he bought it...right before the market insanely rebounded in early 2021 from the COVID shutdowns beginning in March 2020. Most people were not buying when he bought. But investors like Ben did.
- By 2021, the real estate market had appreciated so much post-COVID that he already had A-typical equity in his three Texas rentals. Additionally the interest rates had dropped to 40-year lows and he knew this was a rare and limited opportunity. Because of this, he knew it was time to facilitate the improvements he promised his wife on their primary home in Massachusetts. He did *cash-out refinances* on each of his three Texas rental properties and pulled out $100,000 which he used toward these improvements. These were improvements (new energy star windows and central air conditioning and heating added, interior design updates), not expenses, and increased the value of his home, therefore allowing his *balance sheet* position to stay the same. When something is an expense, the money is spent and gone and the asset side on your *balance sheet* would be reduced. However, Ben's *cash-out refinance* to home improvements example, you are just moving equity rows on your *balance sheet*. He increased the Texas rental

> mortgage amounts on the liability side by $100,000 and added that same $100,000 to his primary home asset value, thus making no change to his *balance sheet net worth (Net worth = Assets - Liabilities)*. Because of the post-COVID super 40-year low interest rates he refinanced to, even though he increased his loan amounts with the *cash-out refinances*, he was able to keep cash flow positive on all three Texas rentals. This is the magic of understanding finance. If this seems confusing or overwhelming, I may not be explaining it well. It's not that hard, you just have to learn the language and practice speaking it.

Ben told me he loved watching his bank account balance increase by about $500-$700 a month, thanks to his rental property cash flow! Also by 2021, he was ready to take a deeper dive into one of the *4 ways to make money in RPI* and Pillar #2 in *The First 4 Pillars*...Tax Strategy. The most underutilized benefit to having an *active & properly structured business* is Tax Strategy. Let me repeat, the key to utilizing tax strategy to the max, is having an *active & properly structured business*. You probably don't fully know what that means, and I can almost assure you don't, even if you think you do. The reason why I say that is because it's a vast vortex and if you are a normal person like me, you don't know what you don't know on this infinite subject. But the basic component is that you run your rental property business under an LLC and your LLC files its own tax return. Please talk to a CPA or a Tax Attorney. Neither will be as expensive as you think and most do first time free consults. A good tax attorney or CPA makes you back whatever you spend with them many times over. This thinking is a consumer to investor shift. Good partners like tax attorneys are never expenses, they are always investments.

Ben was ready to start *The First 4 Pillars* in his *RPI Business* and set up his Texas LLC in 2021. I referred him to Evan, the tax attorney I have personally worked with since 2014 and who I refer many of our RPI to. You can work with a Tax Attorney who is not licensed in your state because taxes are federal. But if you ever have to go to court in your state, obviously they couldn't represent you. That is called making a business decision. I made it and Ben did too. Before Ben had an LLC, he had an *active* business. However, it wasn't *properly structured*. Once he combined the active part with the properly structured part by setting up an LLC, a part of the tax code was now available to him that he previously wasn't able to utilize as a *RPI Business* owner. That is what the right leadership can do. They know things you don't. And Ben's leadership led him to a very advantageous tax strategy.

He was originally out of pocket about $210,000 with his down payments and closing costs on his three Texas rental properties. Remember, he pulled out $100,000 from the *cash-out refinances* in 2021. Then he got back about the same when his tax returns were amended to his business entity. A deeply important point here. Ben didn't officially set up his LLC on paper until years later so how were his tax returns calculated to shift his rental property income and expenses to his LLC's tax return and amend them from his personal 1040 returns? You can amend your last three tax returns for up to three years from when you filed. So Ben amended his last three years of tax returns, 2018, 2019, 2020 in 2021. Evan was able to confirm his rental property business was truly operational beginning in 2018 (remember he closed on his first rental in December 2017, so 2018 was when he started to collect rent and have mortgage expenses), but just not structured as a business through the IRS eyes. When you only write off expenses through your personal 1040, or married filing jointly 1040 EZ return, the IRS thinks your business is a hobby, not a true business. And honestly many RPIs don't even think their *RPI*

Business is a real business, but it is. They think they only have an investment, and not a full business. A *RPI Business* is a real business just like a food truck, shoe warehouse, appliance installer or plumber. Obviously you might not have as much revenue, expenses or employees as some of these examples, but an *active & properly structured business* is an *active & properly structured business.* You provide jobs. You pay salaries. You collect income. You pay property taxes. You pay sales tax. You will pay capital gains tax when you sell. You hire tax attorneys and business entity strategists, and realtors, and property managers, and insurance agents, and plumbers. These are not consumer activities. These are business owner investor activities. You prime the pump of the economy. You build business. You are probably thinking what Ben did is expensive. To set up his LLC and amend 3 tax returns, cost him about $5000. So with his *cash-out refinance* and amendment rebate, he was just about made whole with the $210,000 he originally invested. This is powerful. To me, Tax Strategy is what powers the sun. And it is so under-understood.

Ben is a top Fox working his way to *Becoming an Elephant*, a net worth millionaire from rental property. The only reason he is not an Elephant already with just his 3 rental properties and his vacation rental is simply because his properties are still leveraged with mortgages. Once the tenants pay down his mortgages he will be. So it is just a function of time. Remember, it takes time to build a pension. He is going to be a first generation millionaire and his year 1 was only in 2018. Double that and he will be there with the equity that will grow and mortgages that will be paid down by tenant rent. Even if he doesn't buy one more property. Remember you only need 4 rental properties and a decade or two for your tenants to pay off your mortgages to be a first generation millionaire. Has a financial advisor or someone savvy in finance ever looked at your current investments and told you that you are on track to becoming a millionaire? I told

Ben this, because it is true. And a financial adviser told me this in 2011. Remember Ben is a normal guy just like you and just like me. Working hard. Making money. Saving. Investing...rinse-repeat. Not to 100 properties, just to 4.

His current plan is to take the next few years to pay down debt from their Massachusetts home renovations. He will keep his super low interest rates on his Texas rentals and when his kids go to college in 8-10 years, he can do another *cash-out refinance* because his homes will have likely doubled again in value, or he could sell them. Maybe he will sell one and pay off the others to get more cash flow and retire earlier, or do Airbnb investing, or perhaps move into one. The point is, he has many options.

This is the point indeed. RPI gives you options for your future. And your future starts NOW. Most people won't have options, but you will. He said his only challenge currently is that he wishes he had a pile of money to buy more property, but he doesn't because he is normal like you and like me. One of the very best decisions he made in his life was to jump into RPI, he told me warmly. He said that if he could talk to his former self, he would say, "You do not have to have every single detail about the real estate business figured out to jump in."

In truth, the punchline is that you never will, and it will all work out anyways with enough time. The *x factor* is always *time.* Accept that you will play the long game and you will win. But before you can finish, you must simply start. How do you eat an elephant? One bite at a time. If Ben, susceptible to analysis paralysis, could free himself from those shackles and dive in, you can too. That is, as long as you are *Willing & Able*.

So what are some more traits of a Fox? They are the scrappy ones. They watch and prepare. In the beginning they may be a little skittish or timid, but once they figure it all out, they have a confidence that drives them to dominate and outsmart the dogs and chickens.

Foxes are generally less emotional and more data-oriented. They are managers who work well on teams and value input from others—the same way Ben recruited us on his team. Foxes are aware that the race is long, and once they identify the starting line, they run.

Many Foxes have run some races before in other businesses or investment pursuits. Because of their inherent competency and speed, Foxes sometimes fall prey to running too quickly and getting ahead of themselves once they get going. Reminding yourself to take it at a reasonable pace, lean on your team, and be solutions focused is critical to a Fox. Foxes work well using *SMART* Goals.

Because a Fox is careful and measured, this sometimes means sticking to what they know for a season. There's nothing wrong with that. Eventually, though, a Fox will learn to increase risk tolerance and graduate to something like Elephant status by diversifying assets and stepping into new territory. This is what Ben attempted to do in Texas Rental #3, but realized he wasn't ready...and may never be for that type of business model. For some Foxes, they stay in their lane and run the same race forever, and that's ok too. In the chapter to come, we will explore the Fox in more detail and you will see if the traits look familiar to you.

Remember, once you are *Willing & Able*, the secret to getting ahead is getting started. It's all about *Picking your Pathway* and *executing*.

Here is Ben's *Rental Property Quilt (RPQ)*:

Property Name & Details	Fate #1 - 3 bed, 2 bath, 2 car garage (3/2/2) Single Family Home (SFH) built in 2013 with 1855 sq ft.	Fate #2 - 4/2/2 SFH built in 2016 with 2360 sq ft.	Mckinney #3- 4/2/2 SFH built in 1991 with 1732 sq ft	Vacation Airbnb Lake SFH #4- New Hampshire
Year Bought	Dec 2017	5-2018	5-2019	6-2020
Purchase Price	$251,000	$278,000	$249,000	$450,000
Down Payment (DP) %	25%	25%	25%	25
Total Cash to Close (DP = Closing Costs (CC)	$69,258	$73,644	$64,240	$102,000
2025 Value	$341,000	$357,000	$381,800	$750,000
Total Years Owned	8	7.5	6.5	5.5
$ Total Equity Gain	$90,000	$79,000	$132,800	$300,000
% Total Equity Gain	36%	28%	53%	67%
% Equity Gain - Annulized	4.48%	3.79%	8.21%	12.12%
ROI (Total Equity / Total Cash to Close	129.95%	107.27%	206.72%	294.12%
ROI (Total Equity / Total Cash to Close -Annualized Return	16.24%	14.30%	31.80%	53.48%

CHAPTER SIX

Are You the Fox?

Most Foxes buy their first property with the goal of building generational wealth. You will read about some inspiring first generation Foxes born and raised in the United States, you will also read about some investors from less fortunate nations who also believed in the *American Dream* and went after it. The first-generation American investors know the value of what America is (because many of them come from truly poor countries) and aim to maximize what is available to them in this land of opportunities that many of us are fortunate enough to call home.

A key takeaway from every pathway is that inherently to be a RPI, you must be a saver. In other words a theme with RPI is that you live below your means while you are building. For first generation wealth builders, this is a law of success. Live like a pauper for a little while to live like a King or Queen forever. The majority of our Foxes are in their 30s or 40s, married with a couple of kids. They max out their 401K and always take advantage of the company 401k match program. Their consumer debt is low and they like the idea of using *OPM*, good debt, as leverage against an asset to get ahead.

Credit wise, they are usually in the 700-800 club. They might even be renters in expensive areas like San Francisco, Los Angeles or New York, and buy rental properties before ever buying a home for themselves. This is known as a Renter-Investor and is not a wrong way to go about it. Actually a few months before I published this book, I myself was a Renter-Investor, living in an apartment for three years. I bought my *Move-Up* rental property (this will be defined shortly in a Fox pathway) and did an extensive rehab on it over the course of 4 months. I lived in my apartment while carrying out the rehab covering both my rent and my mortgage payments as well as paying cash for the rehab costs. This was my 11th rental property asset to buy and fourth to do an extensive rehab on. I have probably done over 100 lighter rehabs for clients over the years. And let me tell you, extensively rehabbing properties is a whole other book. It's a hot, dirty, expensive, risky, time sensitive business and much, much, much different than the RPI pathway I will be teaching in this book.

Foxes usually have a *FIRE*[6] mindset and diversify their portfolios with other safe investments. For the most part, they want a few rental properties, knowing their entire family financial downline can be changed with $1-2 million in rental property net worth. They are self-starters and know how to make their money work for them early in life. They play the long game and understand *TVM* is working for them. Conversely, if you don't invest your dollars, they will be inflated due to inflation reducing the value of money.

While this is our main Fox prototype, don't be discouraged if you don't fit this mold to a tee. You might fit better in another animal personality category *or* you might be a hybrid. For example, you might not have a high credit score, but you identify with every other component. Or maybe you check every box, but you have large consumer

6. Financial Independence, Retire Early

debt. The goal here is not perfect classification, but *approximation* so you can *Pick Your Pathway* and get started and/or grow your portfolio.

Unfortunately, many Americans do not think about the long game whereas Foxes are almost hard-wired to think about it. In a way, this is an immigrant journey for you even if you were born in America, because you will be first generation wealthy. Let's learn from some other Foxes in the pathways to follow. Remember to bookmark the pathways that you feel could be your *Version 1 (V1)* plan because if you are *Willing & Able*, the secret to getting ahead is getting started.

SONNY

Diversity Against the Stock Market Pathway

Sonny was born in a tiny town in India —a village so small one could walk from one end to the other in flip flops. Seriously, it is 6 square miles and has about 40,000 people in it today. For better opportunities, his father would later move the family nine hours away to a huge tech capital—to start his own business of selling microprocessors. When I asked Sonny if he grew up middle class, he replied, "I thought we were middle class until I realized I was the only kid with a car in college, then I realized we were more upper middle class, but not rich. My parents were both focused savers."

Being a computer science whiz like his father, Sonny considered working in the family business after getting his bachelor's degree in India. With encouragement from his folks to "make it on his own" he moved to the U.S.A. to obtain a master's degree at the University of Texas at Dallas. This was 1992 and his father gave him a loan of $6,000 to begin his new life abroad, the equivalent of $13,000 today. Would you move halfway around the world with $13,000 in your pocket? That's pretty bold. And we all know that many people have done it for far, far less. He recalls working three jobs to support himself through his master's program and focused on putting money aside as he studied. In the morning, he had a job in one of the dorm cafeteria's flipping burgers to prepare lunch for the students, then would rush to his second job at the university's administration office to process patent applications. He would then rush back to his dorm to change into a suit for his third job working for the first Internet Service Provider in DFW called Unicon.

When he graduated two years later, he had a paid off Master's Degree and had $50,000 in his savings account. Because his parents were savers, he picked up the same habit, but took it to the next level. He aimed to buy everything with cash as he grew up, avoiding loans altogether. That went for cars, houses, and investments. He is a rare Fox in that he bought his primary home and his two investment properties in cash. For his age at the time, 40, it's extraordinarily rare to have hundreds of thousands in expendable cash on hand. He sacrificed a lot of time and desires and stuck to a very high savings rate to yield these results a couple of decades later. Remember how I taught you that your future self would thank you if you saved in your present? Well, check mate.

Let's do some basic math. During his three jobs, let's be conservative and say he made $800/week at 48 out of 52 weeks worked in a year. That amounts to $38,400 per year or $76,800 over the two years he was getting his Master's degree. That was good money for a college kid from a tiny town in India. And little did he know that those two years would set his savings values up for his entire life. We all know that houses need a strong foundation...so do finances.

After taxes we can assume he was left with $65,280 to 'spend' over those two years. If he had $50,000 by the time he graduated, that means he spent $15,280 total over two years or $7,640 per year ($13,000 in today's money) or $636 per month. Now to be totally fair, he had a full ride scholarship where tuition and room/board was covered, so I don't want to even hint that every person could do this today. But, I have a notion that many people could live at home during their college years and live rent free or close to it, get a job where you get free hamburgers like he did, drive a 15-year-old car, and shop at Goodwill. For Sonny, we can wager that he lived a pretty minimalist life for that time, but it paved the way to his future financial success. As a young person he had the energy, aptitude and ability to do this. That doesn't mean that at any age, at any time, you can't adopt this mindset and behavior. Many Foxes and Elephants operate like this. It's like a game to them. *The Money Game* and many first generation millionaires have played it. I know I have.

Because of the diligence and care that Foxes like Sonny exude, they typically max out typical investments like mutual funds and 401ks. They typically have a low risk tolerance. This is why when they *pivot* to investing in rental property, they usually buy class A or B rentals in A or B areas. They don't make risky bets on D class communities or flips.

Because Foxes are very research driven, focused and thoughtful in their investments, they can often be the same way as landlords and managers. Sonny was no exception. At one point, a rental property of his was occupied by a professional poker player, who we will call Peter. After Peter would return from Vegas, he would store his cash earnings in a large safe that he kept in the property. One night, a neighbor called the city about water overflowing out of the house and coming out of the garage down the driveway and into the street.

My property management firm was managing Sonny's properties at the time and so I woke up to several missed calls overnight. Fortunately, the city shut off the water to the property, otherwise when I arrived the next day, the house might have floated away. Turns out, the second level toilet somehow overflowed out of the bathroom, down the stairs, through the ceilings, out the back door and through the garage. We think the water ran for a few days before being noticed, as that is how long the tenant had been in Vegas.

After assessing the damage and calling Sonny, he was there in a snap. Foxes are generally not procrastinators. They manage head-on and get to a place of acceptance quickly, refusing to fight and fret over what they cannot control. He was calm, didn't complain, and came with a great degree of focus. He called his insurance company and asked me to work on mobilizing a water remediation team. The key in those cases is to pump out water quickly and start drying the walls and floors to avoid mold and further damage.

The furniture was removed, floors were shop vacced, and industrial fans were everywhere. Sonny set up a little 'office' on the second level where the half wall banister was. From his 'desk' he acted as the general contractor, coming back every day to work with the mold remediation team to get the unit dry and to plan out an efficient remodel where new floors and paint were needed.

Admittedly, if this had been under my watch, it would have taken five times longer as I didn't have the bandwidth to solely manage an emergency like this in addition to the 40 other units I managed, in addition to my real estate brokerage. Because Foxes thrive in project management and building out solutions, Sonny had the entire remediation and rehab finished in two weeks. It was like watching project management as if it were art. When asked about his razor sharp acuity, he replied "I like to be positive. All of us lose some chips in our lives every now and then, it's how we get over it and move forward that matters. I don't like to play the 'I could have done this or that' game. I just focus on moving forward. You can only control how you respond."

If you don't carry this same trait, don't fret, it can be a learned habit. I am living proof of this. Sonny was a role model for me in adopting this mindset. Below are a few mantras you can use to adopt as you build the Sonny mindset:

RPI POSITIVE MINDSET MANTRAS:

- Accept, Adapt, Overcome (AAO)
- I'm grateful for my RPI Businesses
- The glass is always half full
- The only thing I can truly control is my perspective
- I will not lose my peace over anything
- I can start my day over at any time
- This too shall pass
- In the long run this will all work out
- Let Go and Let God
- The Serenity Prayer: "God, grant me the serenity to accept the things I cannot change, the courage to change the things I can, and the wisdom to know the difference."
- I can't ever fail if I never give up, I just pivot
- Perfection is the enemy of good
- ABL: Always be Learning

Beyond Sonny's response, the tenant was just as calm and positive. All he cared about was making sure the safe wasn't water damaged—which it wasn't. He said "Everything else is just furniture, no big deal. I am just glad everyone is ok." I was used to being yelled at by tenants and landlords so this was a pleasant response on all fronts. How you choose to treat people is so valuable. I have found that Foxes always treat people well, because they value them. That is the main reason people like working with Foxes so much because they are just great people.

To a Fox, it's all about failing forward, improving, and growing. Nothing will sink the ship to a Fox because the ending isn't revealed until it's over, and it's not over until it's over. Even if a Fox pays cash for a rental property and isn't required to have a homeowner's insurance policy, like Sonny did, they still have one. In fact, this incident came with an $80,000 price tag which insurance covered almost in full. Because Foxes are risk averse, they follow the rules and the rules say always get home owners insurance on your home.

Sonny's Fox-like response had become a model for me and I coveted it for years. When my apartment flooded while I was on a trip to Italy in 2023, I pulled out Sonny's blueprint on how to manage it. I knew to lead with kindness and calmly accept, adapt, and overcome the situation. I even got a compliment along the way from someone involved in the renovation saying "you are the nicest person I have encountered in an unfortunate situation like this." By being kind to others, did that mean I or Sonny got walked over? No, being kind doesn't mean you are weak. In the end everything works out when you look at it like a learning experience. My insurance covered almost $20,000 in cleaning and replacement cost just like Sonny's insurance covered his flood. What more could you want? Accept, Adapt and Overcome has served me well in this situation and many other rental property unexpected adventures. What will be my take away from this in 5 years, 10 years, 20 years? I will remember that I got a compliment from someone that I touched in a positive way and it all worked out. Trust me, I spent many years playing a very different game which focused on blaming others, resentments, victim mentality, and not trusting my team. This was in my Lone Wolf phase. Fortunately Lone Wolves can evolve out of this phase and happily, I am a success story.

Like Sonny, Foxes have a strong self-worth. They know the value they bring and usually arrive with confidence, not arrogance. Sonny remarks that, "Comparison depletes you. You can end up in depression with comparison. On one end you can feel like you don't measure up with the other person. Or, you can feel like you are entitled and better. Neither are helpful." Foxes stay in their lane and focus on themselves, not how they compare to others.

Foxes are mindful of long term wealth-building, they are also keen on short-term maneuvering. It's usually them-against-them. It was 2010 when Sonny bought his two rental properties in DFW, Texas and that was as far his rental portfolio got to. When I was interviewing him for this book, he mentioned he was ready to sell his two rentals and focus on the stock market more, which he feels is more in his wheelhouse and will serve him better at this stage of his life. When investors want to discuss the idea of selling their rental property assets, I have two questions I ask them: Do you want to scale? If not, then let's sell. If you want to sell, do you have another investment you want to put the proceeds in? Sonny is not in acquisition mode, he is in liquidation mode.

The beauty of real estate investing is the options it provides. You learned about a few in Ben's pathway (*cash-out refinance, Tax Strategy*, *BRRR*) but another very common one is to do a 1031 exchange or liquidate all together. You would think that savvy Foxes like Sonny would know his exact numbers and percentage returns. In reality, he had a very good idea, but didn't know exactly. I wanted to make this point, because if you don't know your exact numbers you are not alone. It took me years to figure out my own and it's an area I am always iterating and growing in. If you are going to be a normal RPI like me and the pathways, then we are all mom and pop small businesses and our books and reports will never look like Blackrock's. I wanted to run Sonny's real numbers in a deeper fashion for him and see what his returns looked like on his two rentals. The exercise was valuable for him and me and I thought it would be valuable for you too.

Here is Sonny's *RPQ*:

Property Name & Details	Townhome #1 - 3/3/2 Townhome, built in 2006 with 1769 Sq Ft	Townhome #2 - 3/2.5/2 Townhome, built in 2008 with 1682 Sq Ft
Year Bought	Jul 2010	Jul 2010
Purchase Price	$165,000	$161,500
Down Payment (DP) %	100%	100%
Total Cash to Close (DP = Closing Costs (CC)	$171,000	$167,500
Sold Value	$401,900	$370,000
Total Years Owned	14 (Sold 7-2024)	13.25 (Sold 10-2023)
$ Total Equity Gain	$236,900	$208,500
% Total Equity Gain	144%	129%
% Equity Gain - Annulized	10.26%	9.74%
ROI (Total Equity / Total Cash to Close	138.54%	124.48%
ROI (Total Equity / Total Cash to Close -Annualized Return	9.90%	9.39%

Fun Fact: I own a townhome in this very neighborhood (that I bought from a Lone Wolf you will soon read about) and so do many of my other investors.

In our talks, I asked Sonny if he thinks the *American Dream* still exists and if what he accomplished could be done today if he were starting over. "Yes," he said definitively, "The USA has been a melting pot of world contributors for hundreds of years which has made our country what it is today. Are there problems? Yes, there are complex problems, but if you work hard and are innovative, it will work. Leadership, maturity, and stability are all traits that have high value in America."

CHAPTER SEVEN

Steve
Following in RPI Uncle's footsteps Pathway

Like Sonny, our Fox client Steve knew that to be successful, he must get the right people involved. Steve watched his uncle build quite the portfolio in North Carolina in years prior and Steve felt inspired by his example. Though Steve lived in Northern California, he was drawn to the DFW region and wanted the Lonestar State to be his canvas. Steve saw what we were doing for other investors and wanted to be part of it. Foxes utilize the power of networks, which is how he found out about our team. Steve liked that we offered a technology focused process oriented around investors like him who were busy working 40-60 hour weeks. Because Steve had a vision of what success could look like thanks to his uncle, we were there simply to help him build a structure, get started and *execute* it. Trust me, there is a team like this in the market area you are interested in. We live in a digital age and agents/property managers have figured out how to communicate with RPIs virtually by now.

He was one of the easiest Foxes we have had the privilege of working with. His uncle's pathway provided him another level of security and confidence that many first time investors simply do not start with. Basically, he had already been inside the matrix and was just looking to mimic what his uncle had already built. A quick tip for skittish Foxes struggling to get started: call up that proverbial uncle, friend or cousin who is in the game and pick their brain. Not the 'I caught a fish this big' kind of contact you have, but the humble, honest, real, long term, insightful, Team You contact you have. You have one. I am pretty sure you do. But if you truly think you don't, then your rental property specialist realtor will be that person for you. Steve, however, came with some insight because of a relative who had paved the way.

A few months after being introduced to Steve in 2018, we helped him close on his first rental property and Steve was excellent at staying in touch and being serious about building his business after. We offer our RPIs check-in points with us after they close and believe it or not, very few investors take advantage of our check-in offer. However, Steve did. The first year after our investor closes, we give them a framework called *The First 4 Pillars.* It is one activity per quarter to help them set up their new business. Many investors miss the big picture in what setting up a rental property portfolio really means, in that you are actually setting up a business. For other investments that is not the case, but it is absolutely the case here. I built *The First 4 Pillars* because for years my business was a messy-mess and an afterthought. Like anything in life, you get out of it what you put into it.

This is just a framework, some follow it exactly, others take their time like Ben did in setting up his LLC structure years later. Remember, the secret to getting ahead is getting started not just in buying property but taking your business seriously. And you only can get the most out of it if it is an *active & properly structured business.*

You can't make a wrong decision in *The First 4 Pillars*, the point is that you make them and start building a top of mind structure.

THE FIRST 4 PILLARS:

1. **BUSINESS ENTITY STRATEGY-** Decide if you are going to put your property(s) into a business entity (e.g. LLC, Series LLC, etc.) and if so, get that set up. Most business attorneys can set up basic LLCs. I always say one of your first business decisions you will make is to decide if you will keep your rental property(s) in your personal name (if you took out a residential mortgage) or move it/them to an LLC. Like all substantial decisions, this has pros and cons. If you keep them in your personal name, you open up your liability to your personal assets being exposed if anyone ever sues you. However, if you set up an LLC and move the title of your property to the LLCs ownership, then you expose yourself to the risk of the due on sale clause being triggered. That is a term of your loan that stipulates you are not allowed to change the title ownership name without paying off your loan. If the due on sale clause is triggered, then the entire balance of your loan would be due in full in 30 days. Terms vary, but more or less this is what it says. THAT IS SCARY I know. But these are the types of decisions business owners make. Even if you don't own a business you have made decisions like this to some degree, I assure you. Take the job or don't. Move to the new state or don't. Marry the person of interest or don't. In a way these decisions are in the same category. They are all risky and calculated decisions with potential long term gains or losses. And most normal people like you and me are probably not equipped to make them. You just do your research, seek appropriate counsel, discern which pathway gives you peace,

make a decision and move forward. This decision is a highly personal one and there is no right or wrong answer, so your job here is to make a decision and like Sonny says, "don't play the should've, could've game." Make a decision and go with it. Pro Tip: When filing a new business entity, you need to have your business name decided upon. We always suggest thinking of at least 3 names to choose from in case your #1 choice is already spoken for. This saves you time and disappointment from going back to the drawing board after contemplating, falling in love with, deciding upon 'the one' only to find out it's taken. Additionally use a name that has some anonymity behind it. Don't pick your name, the house address or other identifying characteristics and always pick something you can easily say and spell. I know it sounds like common sense... but hey, thought we would mention it.

2. **TAX STRATEGY-** What is the largest expense you have? It's income tax. Think about it. You pay the most to the IRS. Owning an active & properly structured business helps you mitigate that as the tax code was written to help entrepreneurs build businesses because businesses create jobs. You are creating jobs. With every rental property you buy you are customarily hiring a real estate agent, a lender, a loan processor, an underwriter, an appraiser, an inspector, a title company escrow officer, their assistant, the title insurance company, the listing agent (because they only get paid by the seller when you buy), the home warranty company, the leasing agent and property manager, the professional photographer they hire, an insurance company. You might also be hiring additional inspectors like plumbers, electricians, locksmiths, flooring vendors, painters, handymen, tax attorneys or CPAs, business entity attorneys, and bookkeepers. In almost every traditional rental property transaction, there are at

least 10 jobs YOU are creating. Since it is your business and you take all the risk, you should get all the tax reward, just like the company you work for does. Pillar 2 is about accepting this exciting responsibility and starting to take action in the income tax benefits that are now available to you. It is time to start researching Tax Attorneys and CPAs who work with small businesses. Don't let this be overwhelming, it's worth the time. Another huge attribute of setting up your LLC is to take advantage of the Tax Strategy opportunity. As discussed in Ben's pathway, when the tax attorney switched his rental property income and expenses from his personal return to his business return, a huge financial opportunity became available to him. You want to shift from a reactive mind (Ugh, taxes are due I have to organize my receipts) to a proactive mind (let me plan for the best tax strategy this year). Savvy business owners treat tax strategy as an ongoing, active filter. Because the IRS tax code is thousands of pages long, they hire a professional. The easiest way I would describe the difference between a CPA and a Tax Attorney is typically an CPA is trained in GAAP which stands for Generally Accepted Accounting Principles and they typically work with the majority of the public. Tax Attorneys have a law degree and specialize in the law of the IRS Tax Code. This is a HUGE shift in thinking for our traditional W-2 mindset clients, which is the majority of those we work with because many only see RPI as an investment and don't see it as a business as an entrepreneur. So it takes a minute for them to shift their thinking. It can take a decade for many to shift to the mindset of an entrepreneur from a W-2, so we encourage shifting your mindset 10% per year. Remember the reason most of our clients build their portfolios is because it will be their income or their 'mailbox' money upon retirement... or possible early retirement if they play their cards right! The point I am trying to make with Pillar 2 is that you are officially out of the Turbo Tax phase of your life. The money you spend on your Tax Attorney or CPAs services is not an expense, it is an investment and you will get a ROI. And if you feel 'guilty' that you will be paying less income taxes than your non-business owning peer or feel like you are not doing your part for America, know this: you, my friend, will be paying plenty of taxes...just not income taxes. You will now be paying more property taxes, sales taxes on supplies bought at Home Depot, taxes on vendors materials and labor in some states, capital gains taxes when you sell, payroll taxes when you start paying yourself, your kids and your spouse, and more estate taxes on our larger than average estate when you die. It's a shift so find your new tribe to discuss this new ideology with and do not, I repeat do not, take advice from people that don't play in your sandbox.

3. **BOOKKEEPING & ORGANIZATION**- Create a physical or digital organizational system, set up important accounts like a business checking account, and get your bookkeeping plan set up. It doesn't need to be anything fancy. You can use Quickbooks, hire a bookkeeper, use a fintech app, or go with a good 'ole fashioned spreadsheet. The key is we don't neglect this. This can be the boring part for many of us entrepreneurs, but the best entrepreneurs are the ones who truly know their books. This pillar is probably the most neglected by small business owners, so we teach our clients to adopt a finance foundation and practice early. It's all about building good habits and processes because you measure what you manage. Getting into a rhythm of monthly or quarterly bookkeeping is an excellent plan. Take your monthly property management statement and type in the income and expenses by line item into your spreadsheet or software

platform you chose. Then add in your other business direct expenses like your principle and interest payment (remember your principle payment is not an expense it's a balance sheet asset), your property tax monthly estimate, your property insurance monthly estimate, HOA, etc. Then you can add your indirect expenses. For example, if you spent $1400 to set up your LLC (Legal Expense), a business development retreat you went on to brainstorm how to grow or refine your business (Business Development Expense), or the cost of buying this book (Education Expense) you can add those expenses to your RPI P&L.

4. **ANNUAL PORTFOLIO CHECK-UP-** A simple way to do this is to keep a notes page on your phone or an ongoing word doc to take notes as they happen. You will type in things like HVAC repair on Oct 26 that cost $350, the property was originally listed for lease at $2200 May 3, 2-total applications, approved tenant and they moved in June 20 for $2200 with a signed 2 year lease, or remember to go over spring maintenance plan. Because trust me, you forget those things. Each year, it's a good practice to evaluate how the year went financially and logistically to determine if you need to make any changes or improvements for the next year. Maybe year two you want to work on upleveling your tax strategy, shop around for different insurance rates or terms, or increase or decrease your rental property acquisition plan. Evaluation is key! This is an active business and like any active relationship, you get out it what you put into it. After all, you are building your future here, so shouldn't it deserve at least an annual review? There is zero percent chance you don't have at least 1 hour a year for this annual check up.

We like to recommend you take 15 minutes a day or a couple hours a week for your first year to set up *The First 4 Pillars* in your new *RPI Business*, committing your time to shifting into the business owner mindset. You can speed it up or slow it down based on your goals. But the goal is to shift, and Steve understood this and took it seriously.

He was diligent in setting up his new rental property business and taking us up on our Annual Portfolio check-up offer. He also connected with us each April when property tax assessments came out, asking us to run comps for him to see if there was an opportunity for him to challenge the appraisal district's value assessment. Basically he understood that there was a bigger picture here than just transacting on one rental property and being done. He wanted to maximize his opportunity.

He was ready to buy his second investment property a little over a year after the first and we kept it in the same county, but a different city. The second property was a little older, but in a more established city. That is how we chose to diversify his portfolio a little bit. Originally he wanted to buy his second property a year after his first, by then he was engaged and his wedding was coming up so we pushed back the timeline for his second purchase by 4 months. We encourage clients not to make big real estate decisions if their focus is on another life milestone (new job, marriage, baby is coming, a move, buying their personal house, long term international travel).

By the time he was ready to buy property #3, we hit 2020 and everything paused. When I checked in with him in April 2020 with a COVID market update he replied with "COVID is a reminder why I picked this market [DFW] to begin with: great demographic trends and diverse economy. I'm using this time to double up on my metro area knowledge...even more." We stayed connected through this uncanny year and he refinanced his personal residence in California and started his refinances on his two Texas rental properties to lock in super post-COVID interest rates. He was then ready to focus on his new acquisition, but not the kind we discuss in this book. His most valuable asset yet...a new baby girl.

Steve is and was such a great Fox. He made the Fox-like decision to plug into a team and leap. Most of our Foxes stop at 1-4 rental properties and see them as a "set it and forget" investment—similar to a mutual fund. When you hire a great team, you don't live in your market, and you buy A/B properties, it is similar to a low maintenance mutual fund.

Here is Steve's *RPQ*:

Property Name & Details	Fate #1 - 3/2/2 SFH built in 2015 with 1510 Sq Ft	Rockwall #2 - 4/2/2 SFH built in 2016 with 2360 Sq Ft
Year Bought	Mar 2018	Aug 2019
Purchase Price	$214,500	$220,000
Down Payment (DP) %	25%	25
Total Cash to Close (DP = Closing Costs (CC)	$58,228	$58,406
2025 Value	$294,000	$312,500
Total Years Owned	7.75	6.25
$ Total Equity Gain	$79,500	$92,500
% Total Equity Gain	37%	42%
% Equity Gain - Annulized	4.78%	6.73%
ROI (Total Equity / Total Cash to Close	136.53%	158.38%
ROI (Total Equity / Total Cash to Close -Annualized Return	17.62%	25.34%

CHAPTER EIGHT

Move-Up Pathway

This is one of my favorite pathways because it's honestly the most accessible to the masses and it is how I started. Typically with the *Move-Up* pathway, investors make smaller incomes allowing them to put down smaller down payments and are typically younger. Basically they have more time and less money. We started calling it the "*Move-Up*" pathway to help want-to-be investors buy investment properties with lower down payments.

MOVE-UP PATHWAY:

Buy a first home with the primary goal of it being an investment property. Because it is owner occupied the down payment requirements are much less. When a buyer puts down less than a 20%, the loan would have *Private Mortgage Insurance (PMI)* which reduces the spread between expenses and income. But PMI will automatically fall off once the property has 20% equity, usually within 7-years based on the amortization schedule of the loan. If the market value of the property increases 20% or more before the 7-years, then the owner can work with the mortgage servicer to get an appraisal and if the house has 20% or more in equity the PMI will drop off.

1. After 1-2 years+ of living in property 1, the buyer can start the search to buy property 2. Once they close on property 2 and move into it, the first property is now turned into a rental and that is now property 1 in their rental property portfolio. The goal is to buy property 2 with as little down as they can. The time frame on acquiring properties 2, 3, 4, etc. can go a lot of different ways. If the property acquisition pace is in alignment with an expansionary economic market cycle, it works well because when property values rise, typically rental amounts rise, meaning the tenant's rent can cover their PITI (Principle, Interest, Taxes, Insurance) which is essentially known as your mortgage payment. If you find yourself in a position where you can't cover your PITI with market rent rates, then you can just extend your time living in property 1 and wait for that to happen. Or you can take some of the money you saved for property 2 down payment and use it to do a principal recast on your mortgage. In other words, your *Move-Up* pathway acquisition plan might very well be exactly what you planned, but with real estate investing, be prepared to be nimble and pivot.
2. Repeat Step 2 until you get the desired number of properties and/or are tired of moving.

The *Move-Up* Pathway is extremely powerful and is a very common pathway for many of our investors inside the pages of this book and outside as well. You can either intentionally start with this pathway or *pivot* into it at any time in your journey of *becoming*. Like we qualified ourselves using *Willing & Able* earlier, it is important to re-qualify yourself to see if the *Move-Up* pathway is right for all decision makers. Many times RPIs are *able* to do this pathway, but sometimes, they are not *willing*. I can't tell you how many real estate counseling sessions I have led with *Move-Up* investing gone wrong and deeply wounded clients because of it. It's a serious business and can affect marriages, friendships, partnerships and your peace. If you turn your home into a *Move-Up* rental property, then you have to let it go and shift your mindset and vocabulary. It will not be your home anymore. It will now be an asset in your RPI portfolio and NO TENANT WILL EVER CARE FOR IT LIKE YOU DID AS AN OWNER. Renters are not owners. Period.

I see the *Move-Up* Pathway go wrong when RPIs are Lone Wolves. Check out the Lone Wolf *Move-Up* Traits *grey box* when you get to Dee's story in a bit to check yourself to see if it's your right pathway. Remember if you decide to go for it and *pivot* later, it's ok. The goal is not to lose relationships or your own sanity over it. Remember you are just in acquisitions to build your portfolio for 10 years, not a lifetime. And 10-years is not a lifetime.

If you can live like a pauper for a little while, you can live like a king or queen forever. This means your initial purchase should not be about aesthetics or setting up the perfect dream home. Instead, the entire ordeal should be carried out with a long-term wealth building mindset. Every first generation wealth builder knows this, it is no secret. It is just up to you to unlock the truth. These principles are yours for the taking my friend...so TAKE THEM.

Some *Move-Up* investors build their portfolio quicker by purchasing two-doors at a time. They'll obtain a duplex for their first property, living on one side and renting out the other. For the really ambitious ones, they will buy a triplex or a quadruplex and scale their portfolio quicker. In DFW, there are very few of these types of assets on the market compared to other market areas. Because duplexes are scattered and scarce, you might not have the ideal location in relation to your work, ideal neighborhood, or quality of construction. Many who buy duplexes end up compromising with certain criteria, which can ultimately be worth it, but you must know the risks. Not everyone is willing to make these sacrifices. Sharing a wall with your tenant is a unique experience and one where boundaries must be set from the start. The tenant must be your tenant before they are your neighbor or friend. It can be a struggle for first-time landlords to have tough talks about rent increases or late payments.

Regardless of the growing pains that are a part of this model, it can be a fast way of getting established when you lack the cash is king position. Most *Move-Up* investors do this for a little while, and then get out. Typically we see the *Move-Up* pathway end for investors once they start having to prepare their children to go to school because they don't want to move schools. The *Move-Up* pathway is good for the younger investors who are more nimble and have less moving parts of their lives. Of course this is not true for everyone, just a general observation. And remember the *Move-Up* pathway does not have to be a life commitment. It is just a version of the bigger plan for most but a much easier way for most normal people like you and me to start building our *balance sheet* wealth. Every single home made first generation millionaire has to make sacrifices. Maybe this is a pathway you are willing to initiate.

SARAH AND SAM

Move-Up Duplex Pathway

I met Sarah in 2017 at a Goat Yoga event. We hit it off quickly and while in the downward dog position with a goat balancing on our backs, we scheduled a meetup. I learned that she worked for a medical device company and her husband, Sam, worked in sales for a restaurant supply company. They were and still are both analytical, personable, and pretty laid back. Granted, they were a little more laid back before they started with their first duplex, but we will get to that soon enough.

Sarah's interest in RPI was sparked when one of her clients, who was a millionaire, gave her a copy of *The Millionaire Next Door* by Thomas J. Stanley and William D. Danko. Beyond that, she played Robert Kiyosaki's board game *Cashflow*. These were two *moments* for her that led her to question, 'Could I do this? Could I be a millionaire?' She was intrigued at the prospect. Before they got married, Sam had already bought his first house before the *Great Recession* came to a simmer. He admits he was not really ready, but they were giving out mortgages like hotcakes back then, so 'what the hell' he thought. My boss used to have a joke back then saying in order to get approved for a loan, 'all you needed to do was hold up a mirror under the applicant's nose to make sure they were breathing'. In other words, being alive was just about the only qualification. I could tell you some wild stories, but we will save those for another day.

In short, both Sarah and Sam were pretty green. At their initial *Investor Orientation*, Sarah and Sam shared their initial 2-4 unit vision with us. We qualified them and their personalities and explained the possible hazards of being a landlord to your next door neighbors. Being aware of the risk, they confirmed they still wanted a duplex, triplex or quadruplex. Being handy people, they enjoyed building and repairing. They approached projects with a Fox-like scrappiness. They were ok with older properties and needed a certain area in the south side of Dallas close to their jobs. Their *Buy Box Criteria* was pretty simple and included these above elements and of course a price range. They were pre-qualified for up to $500,000 with 5% down for a quadraplex. Meaning up to $500,000 for a quadruplex and less for a triplex or duplex.

You see, with many residential *30-year fixed rate mortgages*, you can buy a condo, townhome, single family home, duplex, triplex, or quadruplex (up to 4 attached units/doors is considered 1 property). As a result, their financing terms and approval process would be no different than any other traditional loan. Once you buy 5 units or more, you are now dealing with commercial financing. There are major differences in commercial vs. residential financing. We are only focusing on residential financing in this book.

Once they were pre approved, we did their orientation, built their plan and ran the numbers of some prospective listings that met their *Buy Box Criteria* into our *10-Year Rental Property Evaluator Calculator* and came up with an acquisition price and plan for the range of rent payments needed. We then started the search phase and looked at a few, and they took it in, rated them on a spreadsheet ranking system they came up with and went home to discuss it. Rarely does a Fox make a decision out of FOMO, panic or fear. They process, chew, research, and think. They lean more into their investment mind, focusing on the numbers and less on emotions such as 'do they love it'. However, 'do they love it' does creep up. That is what can make the *Move-Up* pathway a wee bit harder. There is more Jekyll and Hyde in you than you think. Yes it's an investment, but it is where you are going to live and you have needs and wants because you are not a robot. You almost have to look at the *Move-Up* pathway as if you were deciding on which apartment to move into. You care much, much, much less about signing a lease for a year on an apartment, because you know intuitively it's short term and doesn't really matter. If you can apply that perspective to this pathway, you can do well. If you can't, you will struggle with the internal debate of being excited to buy your first or second or third or fourth home and wanting what you want. This is not your 'home', it's a place you will live for a few years and leave it. This is an investment. So prepare yourself and define what it is and what it isn't if you choose this pathway. It's very hard to serve two masters. I love it AND it's a good investment is a very hard combo to find.

After looking at a dozen or so properties over a four-week span, they were ready to make an offer. How many properties should you see before making an offer? In truth, it's not about how many you see, but whether or not what you see meets your *Buy Box Criteria*. Some investors devour 40 properties before submitting an offer. Others look at just two and are ready to sign papers. The more focused your *Buy Box Criteria* is, the less properties you need to see. That is why planning on the front end is so important. Abraham Lincoln said 'If I had six hours to chop down a tree, I would spend the first four hours sharpening the ax.' In other words, the more prepared you are, the easier your task is. In the case of Sam and Sarah, we got their first offer accepted and closed on duplex #1 in 2017, then bought their duplex #2 two years later in 2019 and then were ready to buy after COVID, but the seller market frenzy of 2021-2023 changed their goals.

So they have 4 doors (4 units) housed in 2 buildings (2 duplexes), living in 1, leasing out 3. Please note their Return % when you get to their *RPQ*. It is *insanely good*. You will see why it's worth taking the risk to live next door to your tenant if you don't have the 20%+ down payment needed for an investor loan. There is no other word to describe what they did other than amazing. This is more evidence that the *American Dream* is alive and well my friend.

It's offered today and totally available to you, whether you read this book in 2029, 2077 or 2125. This same plan with modern updates will work for generations to come, and we know this because it *has* worked for the generations of the past. In order to prepare for your future, it is a good idea to learn from the past. Do an AI or internet search on the *History of Landlording* to see how old a way of life this is. People will always need a place to live even when we live in space. There will be space landlords, I can almost assure you. Who knows, maybe you might be one. But before we can write about that pathway, you must first start with an earthly pathway. So *Pick Your Pathway* at the end of this book and get started, because remember the secret to getting ahead is getting started.

It should be noted that *rental property equity (unrealized profit)* typically does not increase *that* much in 7 years, but their timing was right, the area was right, the asset was right. And what if they only got a 5x return or a 3x return in 7 years? Or even a 2x return? That is still incredible by all investment measurements. Remember, real estate investing done right is always a winner, it's just a function of time.

This gain, however, did not come without pain, but I suppose every transformational story does. These two had some hard lessons in learning how to live next door to their tenants. They inherited a tenant in their first duplex who was under the age of 20, which was not easy to say the least. Late rent, loud parties, young tenants not knowing how to care for a property and so forth.

As of 2019 they moved into duplex #2 and now have good, qualified long term tenants on both sides of duplex #1. They made a *pivot* on their business plan for duplex #2 and decided to try Airbnb short term tenants instead of traditional long term tenants. Airbnb would not work on duplex #1, but it did and does on duplex #2 due to its location and walkability. It's a strategy within a strategy.

AIRBNB INVESTING KEY TAKE AWAYS:

- Require a 2 night minimum to 10 day maximum stay
- Require 21 years or older tenants (the older the better)
- You will have repeat customers for various reasons and it's great
- Location *really, really, really* matters, just like it does with hotels.
- Beware that the Airbnb laws and rules can and will change in the area/city/county/neighborhood you own a rental in—so make sure you are able to pivot by selling or turning back into a long term rental if Airbnb isn't allowed anymore.

Are they still desiring to acquire more doors? Yes, we are helping them look for their third duplex in 2025, but they have not *executed* anything at the time of our last edit. They had an opportunity to invest in Sarah's company as private shareholders and are considering using their duplex #3 funds to do so. If they do, this is called a *pivot* and because they have choices, they can do so. This is how their *Move-Up* Duplex Rental Property Quilt currently looks:

Property Name & Details	Duplex 1 - Each Side had 2/2, carport, yard, 800 Sq Ft, Built 1954.	Duplex 2 - The right side is a 1/1 and the left side is a 2/2 Built in 1920.	Totals
Year Bought	Dec 2017	Sep 2019	
Purchase Price	$180,000	$460,000	$640,000
Down Payment (DP) %	13%	5%	
Total Cash to Close (DP = Closing Costs (CC)	$29,659	$28,000	$57,659
2025 Value or Sale Value	$330,000	$624,200	$954,200
Total Years Owned	8.25	7	
$ Total Equity Gain	$150,000	$164,200	$314,200
% Total Equity Gain	83%	36%	
% Equity Gain - Annulized	10.10%	5.10%	
ROI (Total Equity / Total Cash to Close	505.75%	586.43%	
ROI (Total Equity / Total Cash to Close -Annualized Return	61.30%	83.78%	

ARE YOU FOXY?

Foxes typically have engineer-like minds and are bloodhound problem solvers. They are observant, smart and can always find a way to the chicken coup. They seek opportunities and carefully examine them. They lead well-run lives and carry a certain intentionality. Foxes are always a joy to work with. Let's recap some of the top Fox traits. They...

- Are heavy researchers, which allows them to build a good plan, work the plan and *execute* on the plan
- Value people in general as well as the people they choose for their team. They usually nurture long term relationships.
- Are loyal to that team, as long as the team is doing a good job for them
- Trust, but verify
- Understand the long game and don't sweat the small stuff too much...*and it's all small stuff,* by the way.
- Commit
- Are process oriented
- Focus on things they can control
- Are realistic
- Don't spend much time stuck in the past, they accept, adapt and overcome quickly.
- Are "A" clients (see below)

Foxes are the majority of our clients and what we call "A" clients. After closing we generally classify our clients as A, B or C clients so we can learn and improve our process, systems and value. If a client had 1 out of 3 traits, they were C clients. If a client had 2 out of 3 traits, they were B clients. And if they had 3 out of 3 traits, they were A clients.

A, B, C CLIENT CRITERIA:

1. **REFERRED WITH VALUE-** This typically means someone we know, a past client, a friend, a friend of a friend, or someone from our sphere or partnerships. Basically whoever referred us already validated us as a specialist in this field and the client comes to us with a certain level of trust. This could also mean they found us online through a niche blog we wrote, story we told, or meeting we attended. Once the trusting connection is made, then it is up to us to perform and carry out what is expected of us. As long as we do, they trust us and will let us lead.
2. **ACQUIRE WITHIN 6 MONTHS-** *They are ready to acquire within 6-months.* This means they agree to a set timeline, usually about 6-months or less. Clients without a firm or agreed upon time frame are typically not motivated and time-bound to execute and they wait for 'the perfect property' or 'the perfect market' or 'the perfect feeling' which never comes (this is the world Goldfish live in a lot of the time). If they are getting married, expecting a baby, changing jobs, going overseas for a few months or have some other significant life event happening, we suggest they wait to buy their rental property investment after these. They need to be present physically and mentally.
3. **PLAY BY OUR RULES-** If this trait is missing they are the most difficult clients and there is the most tension (enter the Lone Wolf personality...coming up next). We usually can weed these out in our initial orientation. Either we avoid working with them altogether, or we don't work with them a second time. Sometimes we go against our better judgment and miss the red flags. Some things, like nervous breakdowns, are just not worth it.

Our Foxes usually have all three, as well as our Elephants. It's worth noting that almost all of our Elephants in this book are first generation Elephant Millionaires. Some Elephants outgrow us, but that is to be expected because Elephants need a big area to roam in whereas Foxes only need a small hole.

Foxes find their niche, set the parameters, measure carefully, and *act.* They aren't looking to quit their jobs and build the next Berkshire Hathaway tomorrow, but they also aren't setting weak, modest goals. They know what they want and partner with a *RPI SME* to plan out their path. Most importantly they *execute* on the plan, give it a decade or two and voila- it worked. I wish I had become a Fox sooner, my life would have been more enjoyable and peaceful on my way up. Let me encourage you to consider stepping into your inner Fox as soon as you can if you find yourself in the Lone Wolf-dom mindset or swimming in circles around your tank as a Goldfish. Foxes just seem to have a better life, happier vision of their future, are kinder, more things attract them and people pick up their phone calls. I don't know about you, but that sounds like a pretty good life on the way to *becoming.*

CHAPTER NINE

Top Lone Wolf Pathway

Quick Description: The Lone Wolf is the DIYer, usually to a fault. They don't trust or value others and micro-manage. They are typically not very loyal. While this animal could and should be in a thriving pack, they are often Lone Wolves, not mixing well with a team, which can be costly.

After studying investors and clients for the last two decades, I feel that most Lone Wolves don't actually want to be alone. In fact, they really want to be in a pack— they just don't know how. Their style of business is usually rooted in lack of trust. Most people, even introverts, do not wish to exist alone on a desert island. We biologically, physiologically, emotionally, sociologically and spiritually are just not wired for isolation. We are communal beings by design. If you spend your days fighting for elbow room on a subway in New York or walking space on a sidewalk in Buenos Aires—a desert island might sound appealing for a while. But at the core, we were made to dwell with the right people. The right people are an asset, not a liability. Why do you think solitary confinement is considered a top punishment in prison?

Lone Wolves would benefit by implementing the principles of oxen yoking. Oxen were used to plow fields and move large objects before machines were built during the industrial revolution. A yoke is a wooden frame by which two animals, such as oxen, are coupled at the neck for the purpose of pulling a heavy load. Janet Pope lays out the oxen yoking principles for us below:

OXEN YOKING PRINCIPLES:

- Two animals work side by side in order to carry a load that one can't carry alone. If the load is not heavy, a yoke is not needed.
- A yoke makes independence impossible. You can't go your own way.
- Typically a young, untrained ox is yoked with an older, trained ox. The younger learns from the older.
- If a trained ox can pull 5,000 pounds and an untrained ox can pull 2,000 pounds, together they can pull 10,000 pounds—much more than the sum of the two.
- Over time, the untrained ox becomes trained and the two begin to walk in-step with each other. Then they can pull 15,000 pounds.[7]

Once I learned about this principle, I was able to discern who I wanted to be yoked with. It just made sense. There is much confusion in this world, understanding the yoking principles brings clarity.

Lone Wolves typically do not operate within these principles. They don't value who they are yoked with and are often pulling in different directions, on a different schedule, with little respect for the carriage driver's experience or the ox they are yoked with. Basically, Lone Wolves think they know best, even when they have

7. Pope, Janet. "A Yoke? What's That All About?" *Janet Pope*. November 30, 2013. https://www.janetpope.org/a-yoke-whats-that-all-about/.

never done it before. They would not agree with this, but these clients are the hardest to work with and hardest to feel like you are doing a good job for.

They do their research not to learn, but to try to discount what you tell them. They are the WebMD people who 'know everything about their self-diagnosis,' yet still go to the doctor and tell the doctor what is wrong with them. Foxes are of course researchers too, but they are more of the trust-but-verify type. And honestly Goldfish would be served better by doing more sound research before beginning.

Before you think I am bashing this sector of individuals, I should note, I myself am a Lone Wolf in recovery, trying to be more like my Fox and Elephant role models who are humble, kind, delegate well, operate in long term relationships and treat people well. Some of our Elephants actually came from a Lone Wolf background as well. Many of us have parts of all of these animals. My Lone Wolf years were lonely years for me and I spent much time doing double work and spreading myself thin which led to burnout...no friends...and no fun. It's a much more joyful life to work with and trust the right people. If you trust that everything will work out and play the long game, it pretty much will.

TOM

Buy 1 rental & burn your relationships Pathway

When I met Tom, it was clear from the start that he wanted to lead every step of the way. An inborn sense of leadership is not a bad thing, except that he was engaging seasoned professionals and he himself had never bought an investment property before. Our advice was generally thwarted, but he would pull on us to do paperwork. It almost sounds like a sweetheart deal for us, right? Let him do his thing, we write the papers, and then collect a paycheck. In theory yes, but a Lone Wolf rarely makes it that simple. In our experience, the Lone Wolf has a tendency to be double-minded, which is also a Goldfish trait. They might say they want you to be involved and so you plug in. Then after they leave the meeting and go back to their 'wolf den', they send ample changes to the plan. You push back...generally because their plan does not make sense. They want to reinvent the wheel, go outside of the proven process and eventually acquiesce and *execute* their new plan, usually because they want to, need to be right. At the end of the engagement the Lone Wolf is left feeling like they did all the work—which they may have done in a way, but by their choice and due to their control issues.

Could you get to Florida from Georgia by way of Montana, sure... but there is a better, more efficient and effective route, wouldn't you agree? Lone Wolves often think the principle of you don't know what you don't know doesn't apply to them. 'How hard could it be?' they typically think. And the old fashioned, I bet I can cut corners, pay people less and still get the same top notch results I seek, right? Sound familiar? If you were/are a Lone Wolf like me, you have learned these lessons about 10,000 times too many.

There can be many parties involved in real estate transactions from real estate agents to loan officers to loan processors to loan underwriters to inspectors to appraisers to insurance companies to title companies and more. Any of these parties will tell you that a Lone Wolf is a difficult client. There are usually lots of fire drills, insecurity, and a general out-of-flow feeling in the engagement. Why? Because they want to make the rules instead of following them. There is a time and a place where you are able to thrive in being the leader and there are times when you just need to be the follower. If you fight this law, you will not have a good experience. Period.

I will say, a brand new agent without experience, systems, processes, a database, and a team can usually work better with the Lone

Wolf leading, but a professional firm can't and usually won't. When the investor client insists on playing by their own rules to a game they have never played before, it is almost always no good for all parties and doesn't usually end well with warm fuzzies and 5-star reviews.

Tom lived in California and like our other investors, wanted to buy his first rental in the DFW area. I could see from the start that playing by the rules was not his natural instinct, but he had been referred to by a sound client and I was idealistic in my outlook. In truth, some investors might look like a friendly dog from a distance, but up close you see snarling sharp teeth and a feral approach to everything that reveals they are a Lone Wolf.

We did his *Investor Orientation*, and the tension was already high. He wanted to be in control and spent more time challenging us on why our process, building the plan first and then searching, was what it was. Was it useful drilling us on those questions? You tell me? If there are successful results that were shared, then there is proof the process worked. Trust me, it's ok to have questions. Ask away. That is not this. It's the skeptical lens that Tom saw the world through that was not valuable to the relationship. Isn't it flawed thinking to think you know how to do something that you have never done before? And if that is the case, why did you hire someone to help you? If you require changes to their trusted and tested process, then how can the results be guaranteed or expectations be set by the leader? Why would you want to change a proven process when you have no basis or understanding of future outcome? Classic Lone Wolf ideology.

For some reason, both Tom and I decided to move forward and we started working together to find his first investment property. We found one in McKinney and after a tough negotiation on atypical points of contention, we went under contract. When the inspection report came back on the property, it was pretty typical. It was a less than 20-year old home in great condition priced at $275,000.

When we denote a property is in good condition, we usually are not talking about the cosmetics, we are talking about the bones in 7-specific areas. These are the 7 main structural or major mechanical elements that we are looking at:

7 MAIN INSPECTION POINTS:

1. Foundation
2. Roof/gutters
3. HVAC (Air conditioning and heating system)
4. Electrical
5. Plumbing
6. Fence
7. Grading and Drainage and sprinkler system

These are the main areas we focus on when discerning what to negotiate with the seller. It is similar to if you have ever bought a used car. There might be a small tear on the driver seat, marks on the dash board, small crack in the window, creaking back floorboard, smeared lipstick stain on the passenger seatbelt, and even a few dents from light hail ... .but it is a used car. What are you concerned the most about? The engine, the carburetor, the air conditioner, the power steering and the gas gauge working right? That is very similar to how buying a used property is. You will inherit some things. But the main stuff works and that is what matters. Most reasonable people understand that....Lone Wolves...not so much. Even with some wear and tear, there are several generations of life left on the property.

All properties, even brand new construction, will always have something to be addressed on the inspection report. Why? Because houses are not made in a factory, but instead by human hands, built on site and are exposed to the weather elements. There will be a crack in the sheetrock here, a missing piece of weather stripping there, an unlatched door, a dripping faucet upstairs, an unlevel floor or door frame, or a broken window seal in the living room.

In Tom's case, we had a good bill of health in the 7 major inspection areas and it should have been a simple stamp of approval on his side, especially when we and the inspector had greenlit the inspection. Instead, we wound up with nearly 100 (no exaggeration) email exchanges back and forth about the inspection alone.

Lone Wolves, often driven by skepticism and fear, isolate themselves by making mountains out of molehills. Trusting in professional leadership is not in the cards, so they pry and question and accuse all parties to death. For instance, the inspector has no obligation to climb roofs—it's a visual inspection which is the industry standard. This is clear in the report's introduction, had it been read, but Tom bypassed that and scoffed at the quality of the work instead. Demeaning or belittling industry standard practices comes easy to a Lone Wolf. They tend to be accusatory with others and defensive with themselves.

The parties Lone Wolves hire spend a lot of time thinking, 'This just isn't worth it.' During our engagement, I politely asked Tom if he wanted to work with another firm—offering to transfer the deal out so another brokerage could close him. "No," was the reply. A few weeks after we closed on his first investment property, rather than thanking us, he turned his efforts to getting us blacklisted from the online Investor Group in California that we received so many other happy and appreciative clients from. The very group he came from and was referred to us through. And he was effective in getting us removed from this group, which was a primary source of clients for us.

Until writing this, I had almost forgotten about the ordeal and its impact on our company's history. However, I remember seething at the time. A single Lone Wolf can cause immense damage to companies and individuals. We were a small business. A mom and pop operation that worked late hours, weekends, holidays, different time zones, and built a high touch, high care operation with custom processes, systems and calculators to create order in this often chaotic and confusing rental investor marketplace. So instead of a phone call to find a solution or have a meeting to see how we could solve his disgruntledness, he made the proverbial 1 star Yelp review that truly hurt our business and the ability to serve. 100 happy clients, 1 angry Lone Wolf. Lone Wolves tend to be hyper aware of the impact others have on them while insensitive to the cruelty they impose on others.

Now, I don't want this chapter to come across like a venting session or personal diatribe. Instead, let it be a deterrent example. The golden rule stands true and a Lone Wolf, in short, is someone who ignores it altogether. Many times over I could have sued tenants, agents, clients, written scathing reviews, charged late fees, negotiated win-lose deals, and caused a storm for someone else (and been justified in the process). I could literally have been in some court case or another for my entire career. Those who live by the sword die by the sword and I've chosen to lead with kindness and big picture thinking. I have always understood that I didn't want to make it my life's mission to take someone out when we didn't see eye-to-eye. That was not the legacy I wanted to leave behind.

With Tom at the high level, he wanted to buy a rental that met his criteria in the DFW area within a specified time frame. All of those goals were met to a T. If we did not end up being friends—that's understandable! However, Lone Wolves tend to be cutthroat in their complaints.

I recall his wife flew into town in a panic when we were negotiating the inspection findings, in my opinion, mild repairs. What caused the chain reaction of the 100+ email chain and her over-reactive flight into town was the inspector found rat droppings in the attic. Ok...that happens... Not a big deal to us real estate professionals who see it all the time. The first question is are they active rat droppings or old ones? If they are active you treat them. If they are old, they have already been treated. If in doubt, hire an exterminator for a few hundred dollars to make sure. She paid for her flight, hotel, travel meals and expenses, to look at rat droppings and a few other items. I had plans that weekend, but dropped them to pick her up, drop her off, arrange meetings with vendors and property managers, and then do a late night dinner with her to talk about it all over again. I have spent countless full days, weekends, lunches and dinners with clients, but why did this one impact me in such a harsh way? Remember Ben the Fox flew into town for his property tours and I did much of the same activity...but why was that delightful, but this client experience awful?

I remember other email chains that continued on the weekends and at all hours of the night that were similarly painful. To Lone Wolves it seems everything is a re-negotiation. I remained cordial and kind from start to finish. I honestly didn't think I did, but I went back and reread my email replies and I was impressed with myself and even nicer and less direct than I would be today. Sometimes it did take me a few hours to respond because I had to cool down from the constant barrage of him accusing me that I didn't know how to do my job. Ever worked with or for a micromanager? That is Lone Wolf Tom. It sucked.

When it was time for closing, I emailed him and let him know we were closed and funded...the magic words in real estate investing or really buying or selling any piece of real estate. He replied "Awesome, Heather—thank you for your guidance!" With closing done, he now focused on smearing our name.

Lone Wolves will sometimes take you down—or try to. Goldfish might take your time, but they won't take down your reputation. The only solution to working with a Lone Wolf is to recognize it early and either refuse, refer out, or take a beta role where the client leads the engagement and you sit back accordingly. Two alphas doing deals together simply doesn't work.

In truth, after Tom, it was such a blow that we questioned whether or not we even wanted to work with rental investors anymore at all. Can you believe that...one Lone Wolf can make a person question their own calling. As a business owner, when you swim in the ocean all day, every day, you are going to get bit by something every now and then. The question is, how big is the bite? Can you heal up and keep going or has an artery been severed and your business is bleeding out? With Tom, we were able to survive the attack.

To put it bluntly, Lone Wolves feel they know best 24/7/365 and 366 days on leap years. Whether it's rooted in pride, control issues, or general distrust, the actions and words of a Lone Wolf both repel others and isolate themselves. This absolutely limits the effectiveness of that investor, and puts a short ceiling on what they are capable of doing in the industry. Lone Wolves either evolve or stay stagnant. For the Tom's of the world, their Lone Wolf tendency showed up in a desire to take away a path of income from us. Tom ended up costing us an undetermined amount. For me, my Lone Wolf characteristics led me to deep burnout, which came to a crashing rock bottom moment in that 2017 story I told in the introduction. What is your integrity worth? What is your health worth? What is your happiness worth?

If you are thinking, like I used to when I was Lone Wolf dominated, that they are more cut throat in their negotiations and make more money. It's not necessarily true. And how could you even measure that comparatively to non-Lone Wolves? Even if they do negotiate harder and get more, does it really matter if they die with $1.9 or $2.1 million net worth? Isn't it how you treat people and the enjoyable life you have along the way that matters the most?

Speaking of Lone Wolf evolution, is there ever a time when it is good to be a Lone Wolf? I wouldn't say good, but maybe the descriptor is necessary. When you are broke and trying to get ahead financially, you might have to DIY more things. I would try to instill in you to build a mantra like this: I value people and leaders and one day I will work with the best people in the world to achieve my goals. I do not have to take others down or treat others poorly along the way of *becoming*, that is bad intel. We all have something to offer and I desire to collaborate with others to yoke my skills with. We will be exponentially more successful this way. I look forward to partnering with the right people who can help me be more successful than I could be on my own. I don't know what I don't know, but I trust that experienced leaders in their profession do.

He tried to sell the property in 2021 for $309,000 and needless to say, he didn't call us. The listing ended up being cancelled, but the transfer of ownership did occur. The address of that person is back in his northern CA woods, so likely he sold it to someone he knew. If I know Tom, and I do, he probably fired his agent and sold it on his own. Who knows. But either way, as you will see, it is rare for our investors to sell their property quickly. You will, however, soon see a Goldfish pathway with an even quicker sale. But it is not a common strategy, so getting cold feet on a long term investment is not typical of our Foxes or Elephants for sure. A common thread used in sewing *RPQ's* is you hold your property long term. 10 years or more is a good rule of thumb.

Here is Tom's *RPQ*:

Property Name & Details	Prop #1 - 3/3/2 SFH built in 1998 with 1998 Sq Ft (no that is not a typo)	IF He Didn't Sell and Kept it Through 2025
Year Bought	Mar 2018	Mar 2018
Purchase Price	$257,500	$257,500
Down Payment (DP) %	50%	50%
Total Cash to Close (DP = Closing Costs (CC)	$129,234	$129,234
2021 Sold Price	$320,000	
2025 Value		$398,600
Total Years Owned	3.25	7.5
$ Total Equity Gain (from 2021 sold price)	$62,500	$141,100
% Total Equity Gain	24%	55%
% Equity Gain - Annulized	7.47%	7.31%
ROI (Total Equity / Total Cash to Close	48.36%	109.18%
ROI (Total Equity / Total Cash to Close -Annualized Return	14.88%	14.56%

CHAPTER TEN

Are You the Lone Wolf?

Wolf packs in the wild were designed perfectly to work as a community. Naturally the pack identifies the personality traits of each individual Wolf assigning them roles within the pack. They work together to take down large prey, take care of young pups, and cohabitate. Once a Lone Wolf becomes a Lone Wolf, they must take on all the pack responsibilities on their own. The Lone Wolf now must hunt on its own, corner its prey, sleep with one eye open, and take on way more responsibility alone than they would if they operated in a pack with shared roles.

Lone Wolf investors do a lot of the work themselves and refuse to delegate or share in the successes with their team as they grow. As a result, they don't reach their full potential and cannot scale. Most normal people like you and me that build real estate portfolios have real world jobs. If they are Lone Wolves and *also* have real world jobs, they typically burn themselves out. Foxes know how to get the right people in the right seats. Lone Wolves trust their own limited research online more than they trust the real-world expertise of a local professional.

Whether intentional or not, there is a smug and egotistical approach to the engagement with a Lone Wolf. They are routinely annoyed and rarely pleased. Lone Wolves tend to be transactional instead of relational. The capabilities of others are ignored, while their own merits are broadcast to everyone. There tends to be more joy with Elephants, Foxes, and even Goldfish. Lone Wolves rarely celebrate milestones and usually take themselves pretty seriously.

A Lone Wolf tries to play the long game with their money, but not with their relationships. They feel people are short-term and dispensable, but money is forever. The problem is, that ever-so-valued dollar is actually easier to come by when you play the long game with relationships and learn to value others. Before I get too preachy on this, let me give you an example of a business partner and long time mentor of mine, Jay R, who is a master of not being a Lone Wolf.

He seems to continually be at peace in any given situation. Some might say that is because he is financially stable and can afford to be. The truth is, I knew him before his success and his outlook was the same then. Rarely is he upset and pulled away from his belief that in the long run, everything will work out.

In 2007, I helped Jay buy a model home as an investment property. Investors like model homes, because the builder leases it back from the investor as a long term tenant and traditionally pays higher than market rent. I am not sure of the formal term of this type of RPI deal, but we always called them *model home lease-backs*. So the builder is a guaranteed tenant without the need for property management expenses and there is very little risk of vacancy for several years as the builder sells and then builds out the community. Well very little risk, until the likes of the *Great Recession* happened.

It may sound strange that the builder would want to sell their model home and pay rent on it to a RPI, but the reason they do this is to leverage capital. If they have $500,000 worth of a model home, they can sell that model home, take the $500,000 and apply it as a 20% down payment to a construction loan and build 4 more just like it. Paying rent to offset this new financial arbitrage makes sense to them. So model homes typically make excellent investment properties for the time the builder spends in it.

By 2009, builders were going bankrupt, and Jay's model home builder was one of them. The builder was supposed to convert the sales office back into a garage when their lease ended, which is a typical stipulation, but they couldn't. They were also still using the model home acting as the tenant, but stopped paying rent so Jay had to file an eviction. They used the model home after they were evicted and said they didn't. How do we know this? Because yours truly was the investigative realtor and 'broke' in to find evidence. By breaking in, I mean the door was unlocked and I went in, snooped around and found a document on the copier dated after their vacate date.

So Jay decided to confiscate all the furniture in the model home, valued at about $10,000, and move it into a storage unit. And how do I know that happened? Because my sister and I, who was my assistant at the time, were there at 2 am bagging up the knick-knacks and throw pillows in trash bags and organizing the furniture for the movers to come get it the next day.

After the builder found out about this, they basically sent a demand letter to Jay saying he had to return their furniture. Because Elephants decide how to pick their battles, he agreed to do so without a promise of them converting the garage back. Why did he succeed? Because "I play the long game and will make the money back in time. All real estate appreciates. It's time to move on." Jay didn't get the rent they owed him or the garage conversion. So he lost about $10,000 in uncollected rent and $10,000 for the cost of the garage conversion plus the expenses in moving the furniture, storing it and moving it back. But even in a north of $20,000 loss, his Lone Wolfdom didn't come out in an act of vengeance. It was a big lesson for me that I always held dear. He let it go and saw it as a lesson and *pivoted* to a traditional tenant rental and moved on with his life.. He always says we are all just testing and learning.

Did it work out? Jay paid $270,000 for that model home in 2007. It is now worth $573,000 in 2025. That is an appreciation of 112%. Let's just say he hasn't thought about that $20k lesson since 2009. The thing about RPI, and actually any solid investment is if you 'lose' money, just wait for the market to turn around and it will rebound back. Every. Single. Time. All wealthy people know this. They have the trait that most people don't have. Patience. Not having patience is very, very, very, expensive.

On another occasion about a decade later, he had to decide to rehab an apartment building that I co-owned with him as a minority owner. The original proforma for the rehab was estimated at $350,000 and it was supposed to take 6 months. It ended up taking 2.5 years and $1.6 million. We had to do 4 *cash-out refinances* from 2 apartment buildings and he even had to make a personal loan of $550,000 to bridge the loan for us until the 4th *cash-out refinance* was finalized. It all happened during and after COVID to boot complete with mask mandates, supply chain issues, slow city permitting, hyper-inflation, and lots of uncertainty in the market at the time. We also had to fire two other general contractors before I stepped in and took on the role (which by the way I was not at all qualified for) forcing me to move back early from Nashville, TN to Dallas. It was a certified mess friend. The whole debacle is an entire book in itself.

Through all of it, I only saw him lose his Elephant-like-demeanor one time. He still believed in the teams that failed us until the very end and didn't get upset about what happened...because he knows it will all work out in the end. He kept his own boundaries firm and clear, focusing on his job while trusting others to do theirs.

I, however, cannot report the same story. I acted more like a Lone Wolf in this role than an Elephant because I didn't want to do it, didn't know how to do it, and kicked and screamed and complained the whole way. I only got through it because I had a great teammate in Ian who reminded me almost daily to *AAO*. By the end, that lesson made the connection from my head to my heart and I now operate on that principle daily. But I did not like who I was and won't be that person ever again. The complainer, the angry elf, the victim minded Lone Wolf ideology I fell back into on this project. It's just not worth it to do jobs or make investments that don't align with your valuable time, treasure or talent unless you absolutely have to. I thought I had to, but maybe I didn't. I have a feeling Jay would have probably figured it out if I wasn't the GC on the project. But from that painful experience, I learned how to make more solid boundaries about what I will do and what I won't do in my investor journey and career in general. The lesson I learned for the 80th time in my career is to enjoy the journey and not focus too much on the destination. This rehab was a consequence of picking an apartment investing pathway that I was never really suited for. Buying small apartments was more Jay's vision as opposed to mine. I invested with him because I didn't have a clear vision of my own and I had FOMO. My wish is that you leave this book with neither.

In the end I finished rehabbing the building and left knowing that's over and I never have to do it again. Ironically the property manager we hired to lease it out, Jay C, who loves small apartment investing, managing, rehabbing and shop talk tried to recruit me to rehab his next small apartment complex. I told him, not for all the money in the world....well that's a little dramatic. Maybe for ALL the money in the world, but not a penny less. I am not the resource, but I am resourceful and I told him his perfect GC was for sure out there, but it wasn't me. He still asks me every time I see him and I still say no every time I see him.

DEE

Lone Wolf Move-Up Pathway

Dee and her husband, who were retired, decided to turn their primary residence, a townhome in Allen, Texas, into a rental (in the same neighborhood as Sonny two rental properties were in). They bought a lake house a few hours away and decided to move out there full time, but wanted to keep their primary residence in case they didn't like full time lake living and wanted to move back to it. For some people this is a perfect pathway, for some people it is the opposite. That was the case for Dee. Why? Because Dee was controlling and didn't understand how people, i.e.the tenant, could have different thoughts on how to care for a property. Dee could never make the transition from the *homeowner mindset* to the *RPI mindset.* It drove her crazy and she took me and my property management team along with her. Let me just summarize her story right now...she should have just sold when they moved out and called it a day. Her pathway will help you qualify if you are in that camp or not.

Lone Wolf Dee did not want to conform to our processes, play by our rules, or trust us to do the job she sought us out and hired us to do as the licensed and professional property management and leasing company she hired. Additionally, she didn't want to accept the generally accepted practices of how the residential leasing and property management business works. Whenever I would make a suggestion about our go-to market strategy or when detailing a plan for repairs, she was in a constant state of challenging the recommendation. In June of 2013 alone, Dee and I had 5 different email chains on different topics she wanted to nit pick with a collective 35 email exchanges. On what, you ask? Was there a flood like the one Sonny had? No it was her micromanaging the renegotiation of the current tenant's lease renewal. Aren't all investors heavily involved in tenant lease negotiations? Nope. They delegate to the professionals they validate and choose to hire. This is how it usually goes with our Fox or Elephant investors:

> Me: I analyzed the market conditions, inventory and comparables. Based on that, I believe you should negotiate the terms at $1750 per month up from the $1700 current lease term. I believe you should offer to lock them in for 2 years and settle for 1. Here is why I believe this should be the price and the term and this is why (then I briefly explain it). The tenant reply date is due back by XXX. I have attached the comparables reports for your review and for you to see in more detail why I am making these recommendations. Please let me know how you would like to proceed or if you have any questions.
>
> The Fox or Elephant investor: Sounds good, thank you, please proceed.

Lone Wolves...not so much. Lone Wolves have such a hard time trusting and delegating, they can get caught up in their own views of what's important. For Dee, there were 4 main topics she was obsessed about. Pets, us doing quarterly walk throughs with photo evidence for her to see, how quickly or not quickly we responded to her calls and emails, and us coordinating and scheduling quarterly HVAC services. Every time I would send her those quarterly photos, I knew it would be a symphony of unhelpful and unproductive email or phone exchanges for us to reach the same conclusion. I would end with "You can't control how tenants live in your property. We can only assess damages when they move out beyond normal wear and tear. Dee, the more you see how the sausage is made, the more you learn information you can't unknow. Quarterly walk thru's can be excessive for you and the tenant. Is that the most productive and value-added way you really want to spend your time?" But she couldn't really ever hear that, because this was still her home.

Investors that don't fully transition from the homeowner to investor mindset in the *Move-Up* plan make this mistake all the time and I have played the role of *Move-Up* landlord trauma counselor many times. Here is a classic example. The old homeowner turned "investor" thinks it's healthy to drive by their old home and check on the exterior. What do they find? Mismanaged lawn care, an overflowing with neglected mail stuffed mailbox, 3 cars parked in front, and a leaning fence panel. If it looks like this on the outside, what does it look like on the inside, they think. Their mind starts racing. They go to extremes. Their cortisol starts rising. They start adding up the $1000s of dollars it will take to bring their 'home' up to full glory. Those $1000s of dollars have now added up to $10s of $1000s of dollars. We don't have that kind of money. We will have to sue the tenants I guess. How does that work? How could these slobs of a tenant not care for my beautiful home? Are they animals? How could they live like this? How is this acceptable to the no good property management company that we pay? What are they even doing after all? Then they turn to their spouse and project this misalignment onto them. They want them to suffer too. The previously unaffected spouse is now on guard, defensive. An argument ensues because inevitably one party wanted it as a rental more than the other. It's all their fault. Why didn't we just sell the darn thing and be done with it. It's a disaster and everything is going to fall apart, we will lose all of our money and we are going to die.

This is not an exaggeration. Conversations happen just like this. It happened to me personally. I've been the one receiving this very call when I was a property manager, speaking to PTSD riddled clients about this logged memory that happened 10 years prior. It is a real thing.

And let me tell you Lone Wolves tend to be the main manufacturers of such an unnecessary emotional journey. This journey can be less traveled I assure you. I mentioned I am a recovering Lone Wolf and when I start to go down this road, I have to consciously work hard to lean into my Fox and Elephant traits that I have adopted and learned. Everything is going to work out, because I play the long game. I trust my team and in building a business there will be risk. To not risk going down this isolating and stressful Lone Wolf path, I just simply do not drive by my properties. When I am asked to go and walk them by my property manager to assess the condition when the tenant moves out, I ask my property manager to go for me and take detailed photos and send them to me. If I absolutely have to go, I will go. But I try very hard not to. I personally prefer *The Siberia Plan.* For Lone Wolves like Dee, they are hyper-focused on ruminating thoughts of not understanding why the rest of the world just can't operate like them. Dee chose to focus on responses like 'I am absolutely dumb-founded - how can they live that way - when they leased, they said they would take care of it.' And they were taking care of it, but they were just messy. I can't imagine how much of her elderly time she spent worrying about things like this that she couldn't control. At what point in your one wild and precious life do you want to learn the lesson of AAO, letting go and trusting that it will all work out? I wish Ian could be there in your life when you need him teaching you this valuable game changing truth like he did and still does for me. I am not sure Dee ever did learn and the last time I spoke with her was when she was in her 70's. What a sad and depressing trait to die with.

Because Lone Wolves don't know how to delegate and stay in their lane, they don't recognize good teams and processes. Our process was already above and beyond what's normal in the industry, but Dee was always pushing for more. How do I know we had a valuable business model? Because, since I sold this property management and leasing business in 2014, I have been on a quest to find anyone who took as much care as we did. We honestly didn't realize how good we were. We would push ourselves hard to turn a unit in 2 days to prepare it for the next tenant in order to lower vacancy for the owner, do paint and carpet rehabs in 10 days with contractors scheduled on top of one another, we would get multiple bids to find the best value for the lowest price of the repair without the owner asking, we were proactive on communication, we truly cared. Deeply cared. I had no idea how valuable care was, until I realized how hard it was to find it. Doing these extra mile things meant I couldn't scale the business and I would always remain a boutique mom and pop property management firm. But more over, I didn't enjoy being a property manager and honestly it was because of clients like Dee. They wear you out and in the end, it just didn't bring me joy.

Dee always wanted her property to be leased out very quickly. However, she didn't want any pets. We helped her to understand that 80% of tenants are going to have pets and that's something a landlord pretty much needs to accept in order to be competitive. There are precautions you can put in place, like a pet-related deposit, requirements for deeper cleaning, etc. that are considered reasonable. However, Dee went a little rogue with it. She made the tenant put down rubber mats along the first floor to cover all of the wooded areas. The tenant a had superb rental background, a very high credit score, and no pet-related demerits in their history. They were an A-class tenant, paying premium rent who wanted a two year lease with option to renew after that.

While the tenant was agitated by the rubber mat request, they agreed. Every time we did a mandated walk-through, the rubber mats were always a point of contention with Dee. She demanded photos of the mats and if an inch of wood was not covered from a mat shifting during normal use, she requested we contact the tenant immediately. As time went on she decided that she required the pets' food and water bowls be placed in a certain area of the kitchen far away from the wood floors. Of course this sort of rigidity causes turmoil in the landlord-tenant relationships and the tenant is not likely to stay long-term. So why is this a big deal?

A good rule of thumb is to simply follow industry standards as much as you can. Rubber mats, dog bowl placement requirements and photo evidence are *not* industry standard. I get it, it's hard to let go. I dreaded her calls. On the other end of the line was usually an unreasonable complaint or unfounded critique. Finally, I had had it, detailing the extra work and care we exude while also giving her the option of leaving the relationship and seeking property management elsewhere. Essentially I suggested we cut ties, because clearly we were not delivering upon her expectations. She chilled out for about a year after that and decided to sell the property. It was the right move for her because she wasn't willing to shift into a RPI mindset. Ironically, I actually wound up buying her home as my sixth investment property and she was much better to work with on the sale side. So maybe, like me in the wrong role of small apartment rehabber, Dee was in the wrong role as *Move-Up* rental investor. It's definitely possible.

If you think you are a Lone Wolf considering a *Move-Up* like Dee, really qualify yourself to see if this pathway is a fit? Can you shift over to a Fox *Move-Up* if you decide to *execute*?

Do you know a Dee? Are you one yourself? Homeowners turned investors must make a mental shift and understand the emotional complexity of renting out their house. If the shift isn't made, they will drive themselves crazy. Three words must be rallied around: Let It Go. After renting out a property, homeowners rarely move back into it anyways. The average homebuyer will purchase 4-5 properties in their lifetime and it's usually due to major life events like buying the first home, marriage, new baby, upgrading to a dream home, and downsizing as an empty nester. So if you can't let go of your "home" and convert your thinking to that of a landlord, you risk Lone Wolf tendencies and you may not have a positive experience along the way. You might want to accept that your future stress-induced heart attack is not worth it and go find your right investing vertical. For many, this will not be it.

If you still are not sure where you fall on the Lone Wolf-ometer and if you are considering a *Move-Up* pathway, qualify yourself below:

LONE WOLF MOVE-UP TRAITS:

- Can you successfully change your language from 'this is my home, to this is our Move-Up investment property'
- If you think you can't, you can research, interview and hire a boutique property management firm and confess your concerns to them while asking for feedback on how to shift your mindset. Let them know you don't want to be a Lone Wolf and need their help to help you not be. Tell them to give you the good, bad and ugly.
- Can you not drive by every month or week, even if you live close, if you are trying to be a Lone Wolf in recovery and shift from a home owner and investor and into a RPI? Or do you think this shift will be too hard for you?
- If you are married or doing this with a partner, are you both on the same page about your new role as Move-Up investors? If not, is this a conversation you need to have using this pathway to do it?
- Is it a down real estate market or a Buyer's Market and you feel like you have to turn your home into a Move-Up rental because the current market conditions won't allow you to

sell for the price you need/want? Lone Wolves believe they have no choices. Foxes and Elephants know they always have a choice in any circumstance or situation. Now that you know you always, always, always have a choice, can you change your narrative so you are in the driver's seat of your life and decisions?

Remember, for Elephants everything is perspective and if you want to become a RPI Elephant, then you absolutely must adopt the narrative that you control all of your decisions. There is no exception to this rule. If you still don't believe you have a choice or are making excuses in your head about why you don't have a choice, we are going to do an exercise below that helps you see all the choices you would have in this sell, stay or *Move-Up* decision Dee made. Below you will see there are always choices, but the reason above all of those choices of why you always have a choice is because you can also choose how you *feel* about something. If you adopt one of the mind set shift mantras and narratives from the *grey box* in Sonny's chapter then you know you have a choice.

BRAINSTORMING SESSION FOR REAL ESTATE DECISION CHOICES:

1. Do nothing, stay where you are at
2. Turn it into an Airbnb and forego long term tenants
3. Move where you want to go and take a second job to pay for the mortgage on your vacant house that you don't want to turn into a Move-Up Rental.
4. Sell for a loss if you are underwater and move on with your wild and precious life through sub category choices like these:
    a. Off-Market to an investor

   b. To a friend for less than market value without real estate commissions
   c. Do a short sale
   d. Foreclose
   e. List it For Sale by Owner (FSBO)
5. Accept, Adapt and Overcome to the idea that you will turn it into a rental property for up to 3 years and sell when the market rebounds to get tax free proceeds (yes the tenant probably will cause damage, kill the flowers in the yard, and wreck your recent paint job. Expect that they will if you *choose* this choice).
6. Donate the property to charity and take a tax write off.
7. Turn the property into a *Move-Up* rental and stand confidently in your choice to do so because it was the best choice you had at the time made with the most information you had to make it.

And regarding these choices. I didn't say you would necessarily like them or want them, but you do have them to choose from. Some of these are clearly a hard no. But when I make decisions as an Elephant, this is truly how I make them. Once I get all of my choices out on paper, I cross off the clear no's, which gets me closer to my clear yes. I then make a decision and I move on and stand in alignment with that decision as quickly as I can so I am not double-minded. If you do choose to forgo the *Move-Up* like Dee probably should have done, then remember, that every property on earth always will sell in any market or any condition, it will just be a function of time on market and the price the buyer and seller agree to.

Here is Dee's *RPQ* and what it would have been if she didn't sell:

Property Name & Details	Townhome #1 - 3-2-2 plus Study built in 2007 with 1939 Sq Ft	IF She Didn't Sell to me and Kept it Through 2025
Year Bought	May 2007	May 2007
Purchase Price	$165,000	$165,000
Down Payment (DP) %	100%	100%
Total Cash to Close (DP = Closing Costs (CC)	$166,000	$166,000
2015 Value (When She Sold to Me)	$230,000	
2025 Value		$383,000
Total Years Owned	9	18.5
$ Total Equity Gain (2015 Value when She sold to me)	$65,000	$218,000
% Total Equity Gain	39%	132%
% Equity Gain - Annulized	4.38%	7.14%
ROI (Total Equity / Total Cash to Close	39.16%	131.33%
ROI (Total Equity / Total Cash to Close -Annualized Return	4.35%	7.10%

ARE YOU AFRAID OF BECOMING THE BIG BAD LONE WOLF?

Are you in danger of encountering a Lone Wolf or becoming one yourself? Here's a quick acid test to identify Lone Wolf tendencies. The Lone Wolf:

- Values the deal over relationships with people.
- DIY minded
- Is hyper-skeptical, confusing *due diligence* with *researching to prove everyone else wrong*

- Judges everyone else harshly and judges themself lightly
- Doesn't respect industry standards and when things go wrong blames everyone else
- Often makes decisions rooted in fear, which stems from distrust of others
- Can be mean and vengeful
- Micromanager
- Controlling
- Prideful (remember *pride* comes before a fall)
- Scarcity mindset, has a harder time seeing the big picture
- Isn't leaving too many 5-star reviews and furthermore is likely to leave a 1-star review to really stick it to the business that 'ruined their life'

Working with Lone Wolves always made me more Lone Wolf-like and I didn't like it. But you know iron sharpens iron, even if it's Lone Wolf iron. In my career, Pareto's 80/20 rule has played out time and time again. 20% of my clients cause 80% of the headaches, and those 20% are virtually always Lone Wolves. The other part of that 20% are Goldfish...which are coming up next.

Here's the good news: Lone Wolves can be reformed.

While this chapter was a critique of the Lone Wolf, I want to remind again that I am a Lone Wolf in recovery—and on full moons, I can easily be provoked. Trust me, it's an identity that you can and should leave in the rearview mirror. The Fox and Elephant clubs are always accepting applications my furry friend. Both of those animal species can kill, but in our book terrain, they choose not to.

CHAPTER ELEVEN

Top Goldfish Pathway

Quick Description: The Goldfish generally are slow moving. Unable to "leave their tank" they stay within a very narrow framework. They could go after more, but are so specific and limited they often wind up stuck in a small aquarium of their own making. The reason is they typically don't do their research, so when it comes to making a decision, they have a hard time making one.

Goldfish and Lone Wolves have some similarities, but Goldfish are loyal, care about people and typically kind. Goldfish usually do their research by word-of-mouth and soundbites. For example, "I hear this city is good" or "I don't want to buy on that side of the highway." But when you ask qualifying questions like, 'who told you that and when, what was their experience, have you ever been there, did that person say why and how'. The Goldfish come up short. They bounce from one person's hearsay to another person's hearsay and it's really hard to get them focused long enough to commit and *execute* because their research is so shallow. Therefore they have a hard time making a realistic, up-to-date with the current market, well thought out, clear plan and then confidently executing it. They swim around their tank again to see if there are any new possibilities from their community. Foxes do research to prepare themselves and trust, but verify. Lone Wolves do research as evidence that they know more than you. Goldfish do family gathering or dinner party conversational, soundbite 'research' and oftentimes start with the search instead of the plan.

The plan gets changed a lot because they are not confident with the plan enough to make a firm decision. I mentioned I personally have some recovering Lone Wolf-dom in the last chapter, I also have some Goldfish traits in recovery. I have operated in this idealistic, wafey and ineffective decision making aptitude for many years and honestly it was the way I made a lot of my decisions when building my real estate brokerages and investing companies. The reactive Goldfish leadership style has cost me a lot of money and a lot of stress. Years ago as I got more into understanding processes and systems I had a decision making epiphany. It was a process I had learned about when I was in elementary school actually. If you ever participated in the Science Fair, you know about it also. That's right, it's the Scientific Method. Here is a recap of the process:

SCIENTIFIC METHOD

Purpose - State the problem

Research - Find out about the topic/problem

Hypothesis -Predict the outcome of the problem

Experiment- Develop a procedure to test the hypothesis

Analysis - Record the results of the experiment

Conclusion/Results - Compare the hypothesis to the experiment's conclusion

Now let's lay it out again as a real world RPI process:

- Purpose- I want to be a RPI because [insert your '*why*' here] (build generational wealth, cash flow for my retirement, to pay for my children's college, I believe in owning tangible rental property as an investment, diversify my investments, use the bank's money to build wealth, etc.)
- Research- Your research will initially entail market areas, prices, running mortgage calculators with PITI, HOA and landlord expenses, your team of real estate agents and/or property management firms, your budget to make sure you can afford it.
- Hypothesis- I believe I can own a rental property within x time frame with x money in this market area.
- Experiment- Interview and Hire your team, get pre-approved, make a plan with your *Buy Box Criteria*
- Analysis- Start the search and make small pivots as the macro market conditions change out of your control. Keep focused on your time goal. Execute a contract and then close
- Conclusion/Results- Did I close meeting my goals, more or less? What did I learn and how can I improve for next time? Analyze again and run your numbers in 1 year. Decide if you are ready to tweak and adjust for property number 2 then start over again.

Although Elephants might not title this as their decision making flow, they are using it. Elephants have naturally adopted this process or something like it because Elephants operate in a systematic way. Remember this, successful people use processes. That is how they can control and then measure the outcome. They know they can't scale their business or even learn from it effectively without being systematic and consistent in their decision making. This framework keeps them on track to do so. Since I have started making decisions using the Scientific Method, my life has been much more orderly and much less chaotic. I am much more of a big picture person like Foxes and Elephants, which is who I want to be.

If this method brings back elementary school PTSD for you, just breathe and know there is no one grading you. I haven't gone to Walmart one time to buy a trifold foam board as an adult. It's just a quick exercise I do in my phone notes, my journal or card Trello app to see if an idea could work or not. I used to dream up ideas one night and start building them the next day. It drove myself and those around me crazy and within a few weeks or months I was bored with it and the why wasn't strong enough to keep the idea going. Let's just say many things started, but never finished. This is also a Goldfish trait. You start working on something you have not fully flushed out, researched or laid out in the *Scientific Method* to see it's viable. In *The E-Myth*, Michael E. Gerber calls it an Entrepreneurial Seizure. And it is a mess. Now I am all about finishing, executing and being process focused and structured.

It's true, Goldfish appear to be less keen on structured decision making, but man if they are not some of the sweetest clients I have ever had. The Goldfish are usually very nice and sweet and they can make great friends, but they can be frustrating clients. As a business owner, it's not prudent or helpful to work with a client base that takes four times longer to make a decision than the average investor.

Because Goldfish are not usually research based, I've noticed Goldfish are more feelings based. They are usually paying more attention to how they *feel* about an investment property analysis or city, or house layout, or plan we made together and that results in a lot of plan changes along the way, thus making it much harder for them to make a decision. In my experience with Goldfish, when I have presented what they asked for, they move the yard stick. Why? No quantifiable reason usually, just a feeling or a hunch or some new information that popped up for them based on the latest tip they heard. When pressed to give a reason, the reason usually doesn't align with typical reasons investors use when they want to pass. When you shift your mind from a homeowner to an investor, it's all about the numbers. Goldfish easily get stuck in the cycle of looking at a rental property through the eyes of a homeowner. They have a real hard time seeing a house as an investment and not a house they will be living in. Remember, buyer homeowners and buyer investors are two different mindsets and it's very hard to serve two masters.

Being too idealistic is another big Goldfish trait I see a lot for this animal category. They are very rigid and strict on their price, timeline and cash on cash return goals and don't fully understand the macro market conditions which they, us, no one has any control over. To me their idealism translates to illogical thinking thus affecting their willingness to *execute* when the right deal for the current market they are searching in comes along. Many times this inflexibility comes from misinformation they have from their dinner party friend or outdated information from their Aunt Edna who bought property in 1972 and how she did it then. They get stuck on updating their thinking to today's standard operating procedure. And I am not saying 'their way or the highway' type of thinking doesn't work out, but there are better pathways, in my humble opinion. However, if one of our Goldfish 'tales' is your pathway, then by all means follow it. Remember, one of the main goals of this book is to help you *Pick Your Pathway*, so you can get started because the #1 rule of RPI for normal people like you and me is the secret to getting ahead is getting started if you are *Willing & Able*.

LARRY AND LEA

The Ole' Fox to Goldfish Switcheroo Pathway

Larry and Lea appeared to be Foxes when we started working with them, but quickly turned into Goldfish. I made them the top Goldfish pathway because they showed doublemindedness and after spending all the money and taking all the time to acquire, they sold it very quickly without reason or knowledge of what their next investment would be. It happened during the beginning of COVID, so maybe that had something to do with it, but when I pressed, they wouldn't give me a reason.

They very well might be Foxes in their other investment asset pathways, like the stock market, precious metals, gold, crypto, being promoted in their career, or growing their own business. However, I have seen many times where they come to me as a Fox and we get their portfolio off the ground, but they get lost along the way and can't build what they originally set out and planned to build. This is a real risk for you to be aware of. I think it is because this is a long process that takes years and decades to build. And honestly, it is not that sexy and there isn't a lot of commentary around it like there is with the stock market or crypto investing. That is why I am focused on making quantifiable and time bound investing plans so people can have a clear pathway on what they are going to buy and when they are going to buy it and work backwards on how they are going to get the funds to get there.

For example, if the investor wants to follow the *4-in-10* pathway, we start with *The First 4 Pillars*, then I help them make annual savings goals, make a seasonal plan for them to start the acquisition process, follow up with them through the year, etc but many of them fall off course. So they are able to *execute* this plan, but their willingness can fade. Maybe it's for understandable reasons like life events have changed their course, or they really don't like real estate investing as much as they thought they would. But what I find more than anything the reason is "the market isn't right." Well it's really, really, really hard to time the market even for Blue Whale investors like Warren Buffet, let alone a normal person like you or me. Have you ever timed the market in anything you have invested in 100% of the time? Be honest, every fish you catch just simply won't be the biggest. That is inherent and true for all first time generation wealth builders like you and me. That is why most consistent successful investors play the long game.

I built the *4-in-10* this to help investors have a process oriented, time-bound plan with a name to help them *execute* their long term portfolio plan. I can't take full credit for this idea as it was inspired by Yvonne and Mike, (Foxes when I met them, but Elephants now) who bought a property a year every January.

Every 4th Quarter of the year, usually in December, they would rent a hotel and do an *executive offsite*. If you are in the corporate world, you likely know about that term, but I had never heard of it before. A quick AI search denotes an *executive offsite* as a strategic gathering of an organization's top leaders, designed to foster alignment, collaboration, and strategic thinking away from the day-to-day demands of the workplace. It provides a dedicated space for leadership teams to address critical business issues, refine their vision, and strengthen their collective leadership. They applied this to their family investment and future goals ideology and this family philosophy allowed them to fly. They would shape out what their family mission statement was, how they would achieve it and when they would meet these annual goals to support it. They would look at the main foundational aspects of their family life using a variation of The 7 F's.

THE 7 F'S

Faith
Family
Finances
Fitness
Friends
Fun
Future

My phone would ring in early January when their goals included DFW rental property acquisition. Yvonne was no nonsense. They made a plan, defined roles and responsibilities, stuck to them and *executed*. She didn't care about macroeconomics and out of their control elements as the dominant force in their decision making because, you guessed it, they were playing the long game. They had an internal goal as a family and above all they were focused on executing that goal. Mike's job was to focus on making the money, Yvonne's job was to focus on investing it. I didn't say spending it, I said investing it.

It was awesome, peaceful, structured, successful and inspiring to see it in action. It touched me in such a way, I structured my own portfolio acquisition plan like this and so did my little sister Tiffany and her husband. My sister is one of the most successful 38-year old RPIs I know. She has bought and sold rental property properties in 4 different states (Texas, Arizona, Georgia, Florida), had her real estate license in 3 different states (Texas, Arizona, Florida) and her robust *RPI Business* allowed her to be a stay at home mom by the age of 33. Her *RPQ* gave her choices! And *choices* are what make you and keep you wealthy.

What I have truly learned in my own success of RPI and entrepreneurial endeavors is that having a general idea of where I am going vs. not knowing, makes a dramatic difference in outcome. My point is you don't have to be exact and you can *pivot* along the way. For example if you don't like the *4-in-10* and you want to commit to a *5-in-15* (5 doors or 5 acquisitions or 5 assets - in 15 years), then that is one acquisition every three years. Let's say you need $100k for down payment and closing costs for each new acquisition. That is saving $33k a year or $2750 a month or $634 a week. Can you do that? Some of our clients can, some can't. It's ok, don't compare yourself, you are the only one in your race so let's focus on you. If you can't, what can you do? Do you need to do the *Move-Up*? If so, run the math like that and be conservative. If you are conservative with your numbers, you likely won't go out of business. *Always Be Conservative (ABC)*. What does this mean practically? Always have a reserve account, 6-months minimum set aside in a savings account or checking account, for things to go unexpectedly. Be extra conservative on your numbers like assume if the vacancy rate is being reported at 90%, assume 85% or even 80% in your proforma. This core value of ABC will help ensure you don't become part of the 'I lost everything' club.

Larry and Lea had bought their first rental in 2018 with us in DFW and we rated them A-clients full of Foxiness and clear on their mission as first-generation Americans and rental property portfolio builders. It's pretty rare for RPIs to change their minds so quickly, especially given that holding long term is the name of the game. A qualified tenant moved into their rental shortly after closing, signed a 2-year lease and when it was time for renewal of the lease, Larry and Lea called me and said they wanted to sell and not renew the lease. It was August of 2020, so they probably had the height of COVID concern jitters. But that was rare, and I know this because they were the only investors we had who wanted to sell because of COVID. I did a few other investor calls of concern, but all of our investors decided to wait it out. We tried to talk them out of it because their investment was a killer deal. In our *10-Year Rental Property Evaluator Calculator* we estimated that their total average net cash flow return would average 12.62% per year on their initial cash investment of 25% down payment plus closing costs.

Already by mid-2020, Larry and Lea's rental property value was up more than the conservative annual appreciation rate we estimate, which is 3% per year. After running the comps and the seller estimated net proceeds calculator for them, I explained to them that they would only cash-out their original down payment which was about $50,000. But by the time you account for all the closing costs they paid as buyers, initial vacancy and tenant make ready, there would be a net loss. I just didn't see the point in losing money on their investment unless they had to or had a compelling opportunity with another investment as to why. But they could never provide one, they just said we want to sell. It just didn't make sense.

Another reason I tried to talk them out of selling was because their cash flow was over $200 net each month after all expenses and reserve account contributions. That was *extremely* rare for investors who only put 25% down, but this particular property was yielding a high rent to purchase price ratio. Cashflow is amazing because it is the part of the rental property investment that is tangible and helps your cash position or income today. It's like a part time job paying you a paycheck. Cashflow gives you options today, while your equity increase gives you options tomorrow. But it's rare to have that kind of cash flow so early. Cash flow usually comes when rent increases in time. It was a rare beauty of an investment property which is why I pushed back on them so hard to keep it.

Let's take a look at their cash flow numbers on an annualized basis. They received a net cash flow of $2,400 a year off their $50,000 initial down payment. That equals 4.8% ($2,400 / $50,000) cash-on-cash return, not to mention the additional returns they received from the other 3 ways to make money in RPI. We set most of our investors' expectations to just break even—meaning they get a $0 cash-on-cash return back on their down payment for several years in some cases and that is very acceptable and common in blue chip markets like in DFW. That might sound strange to you, but it's a real thing and most every investor we have worked with understood and accepted that as a real possibility. I would almost always explain that at the first *BANT* conversation I had with them. Breakeven cashflow is very typical in the beginning years. As I mentioned earlier, DFW is turning now to a negative cash flow market like top cities in California, New York and Boston. On-Market RPI is shifting more to an equity market. There are still plenty of cities in America and even sections of cities within DFW that are still cash flow markets if that is what you are looking at, you just might have to look at different property classes and areas.

Now let's be clear regarding those initial cash flow break even investors, eventually they will get to a positive cash flow. It will eventually work like a pension or annuity, but it's better, because you own the asset and the cashflow, not just the cashflow as well as the benefits of owning the *RPI Business*. For many self-employed people who don't invest for their future selves or those who haven't saved enough in their 401k, they will have to rely on social security. Every story that I have ever heard about someone living solely off social security benefits always has the same theme: it's not enough. RPI subsidizes your future financial needs and gives you something to enjoy in your life and pass on to the next generation if you want to. And you just need 4 rental properties and roughly a couple of decades to be a millionaire, or whatever the inflated version of a millionaire is in 2055 or 2075 or 2125. It's still going to be a lot of money for most normal people like me and normal people like you.

When an investor is blessed with early cash flow, you have more options sooner. You might use tenant cash flow to pay off the mortgage quicker to increase your net worth via equity, use the cashflow to save the down payment for property #2, or add it to your reserve account, or use it to buy other investments in other verticals, or go on a vacation to Tahiti. Remember, investors have choices. Choices build and keep you wealthy. Investments are the employees of the dollars you make today.

Investing today gives you choices tomorrow. The pathway and plan you choose depends on your goals and if you are *Willing & Able* to achieve them. If you choose to pay off your mortgages quicker, you could choose a *13-month plan* or something like it[8]. However, if your interest rate is very low on the mortgage, you might comfortably place your would-be extra principal payments in a different investment vertical that yields a higher return than the percentage of interest you're paying, thus creating a *spread.*

If Larry and Lea decided to direct their $200 per month ($2,400 annually) cash flow to the *principal* balance to pay off their mortgage quicker, they would pay it off in 19.3 years instead of 30 years and they would have a total interest savings of $65,897.50. With almost all *30-year fixed rate mortgages* you don't have a prepayment penalty. Dave Ramsey has coined this method and calls it the *debt snowball method.* I learned about it over 10 years ago from him and it has been a game changer for me once I started hitting the paydown section of my own RPI plan. There is more nuance to this method than what I am detailing here, so do a google search and go down the rabbit hole, it's worth it.

But Larry and Lea might not ever know about this because they shifted from a Fox to a Goldfish and lost their focus on the long term. They take on a Goldfish classification because they made a plan, committed to the plan, invested in the plan and changed the plan without another new plan, and did it out of fear when COVID happened. When things don't make sense and the client can't explain why they are doing what they are doing, it is typically a Goldfish trait. Successful investors are typically articulate and their decisions make sense with their actions.

---

8. With this plan, a property owner pays one additional payment on their mortgage annually but applies it to the principle. This shaves 5 years off of the mortgage and can yield tens of thousands in saved interest costs.

They had one other Goldfish trait that popped up during the 2020 transaction. There was an outstanding utility bill due, which was high. But utility bills can be unexpectedly high in vacant properties in warmer months. A toilet can run for two weeks straight without anyone knowing or reporting it, someone might leave the sprinklers on too long, or a potential buyer lowers the thermostats during their walk through to 59 degrees and it stays that way for days until we notice it.

Through many emails and back and forth, our firm eventually covered the $300 bill that they felt we owed. Ling thought someone else should pay for the utility services for the last five weeks of their ownership. I don't know why it would ever be anyone else's responsibility to cover standard expenses that all sellers would pay on their own vacant house, but that made sense to them for some reason. These petty disputes are usually the response of someone feeling overwhelmed in a season where expenses are high. It is painful for buyers and sellers to have so many expenses and they usually feel nickel and dimed. I get it.

We always try to help mitigate. With them, we even did a rehab for free—foregoing the 10% general contracting fee (which is now 20%) so they would take less of a loss on the sale. Goldfish and Lone Wolves usually see their risk and expenses associated with their investments as your fault if it doesn't turn out exactly how they think or if something happens outside of the expectations you set. Goldfish come up with an idea of what they think is just and carry it out, until you give in because they won't let it go. But they are usually kinder about it. Lone Wolves will cut your throat over it.

This is Larry and Lea's *RPQ* and what it would be worth today.

Property Name & Details	Prop #1 - 3/2/2 SFH built in 2008 with 1550 Sq Ft	IF They Didn't Sell and Kept it Through 2025
Year Bought	Dec 2018	Dec 2018
Purchase Price	$205,500	$205,500
Down Payment (DP) %	25%	25%
Total Cash to Close (DP = Closing Costs (CC)	$58,500	$58,500
Oct 2020 Sold Price	$225,000	
2025 Value		$287,700
Total Years Owned	1.75	7.25
$ Total Equity Gain (from 2019 sold price)	$19,500	$82,200
% Total Equity Gain	9%	40%
% Equity Gain - Annulized	5.42%	5.52%
ROI (Total Equity / Total Cash to Close	33.33%	140.51%
ROI (Total Equity / Total Cash to Close -Annualized Return	19.05%	19.38%

CHAPTER TWELVE

Are You the Goldfish?

Our average Fox, Elephant and even many Lone Wolf investors see an average of 15 properties and close within six months after doing their *Investor Orientation*. They are very goal oriented and know almost all successful goals need to be bound by some realistic and focused timeframe. Many of these corporate workforce trained investors use some variation of *SMART* Goal setting.

SMART Goals are an acronym and stand for Specific, Measurable, Achievable, Relevant, and Time-Bound goals. The concept dates back to 1981 by a consultant and past director for Washington Water Power Company, George T. Doran. You can use this framework to help you make clear and attainable goals. I have found that being time bound is so very important when meeting your goals. Goldfish are usually delayed by triple, quadruple the standard time frame. When decisions linger that long, you can easily get caught in analysis paralysis, and you simply lose your motivation.

Take this book, for example. When I decided to write it, I hired Nick P who was an experienced full time editor who owned his own boutique book publishing company and had decades of experience.

Why, because I had no idea how to *execute* writing an actual book and doing it as well as I could as a first time author with no formal training. We then set a writing schedule and deadline, and Nick P helped me create an outline of the material which broke into sections that I could then expand on using my subject matter experience and expertise. However, there may be a "better book" by a more qualified author on RPI sitting in someone's drawer, partly done and which will never see your bookshelf. The difference? I would argue, is setting and then executing *SMART Goals*. Remember what Ben cautioned: 'done is better than perfect'. That principle tied to the process of *SMART goal* setting ignites the most important principle of the secret to getting ahead is getting started. *SMART goals* are similar to the *Scientific Method* in a way, because they both create a process driven framework to help you funnel your ideas out of your head and into the tangible. So how do you feasibly set a *SMART goal* you ask? The state of Michigan laid it out in a well thought out white paper they wrote on the topic:

SMART GOAL SETTING:

S – **Specific-** When setting a goal, be specific about what you want to accomplish. Think about this as the mission statement for your goal. This isn't a detailed list of how you're going to meet a goal, but it should include an answer to the popular 'w' questions:

- **Who**– Consider who needs to be involved to achieve the goal (this is especially important when you're working on a group project).
- **What**– Think about exactly what you are trying to accomplish and don't be afraid to get very detailed.
- **When**– You'll get more specific about this question under the "time-bound" section of defining SMART goals, but you should at least set a time frame.

- **Where**– This question may not always apply, especially if you're setting personal goals, but if there's a location or relevant event, identify it here.
- **Which**– Determine any related obstacles or requirements. This question can be beneficial in deciding if your goal is realistic. For example, if the goal is to open a baking business, but you've never baked anything before, that might be an issue. As a result, you may refine the specifics of the goal to be "Learn how to bake in order to open a baking business."
- **Why**– What is the reason for the goal? When it comes to using this method for employees, the answer will likely be along the lines of company advancement or career development.

M – **Measurable**- What metrics are you going to use to determine if you meet the goal? This makes a goal more tangible because it provides a way to measure progress. If it's a project that's going to take a few months to complete, then set some milestones by considering specific tasks to accomplish.

A – **Achievable**- This focuses on how important a goal is to you and what you can do to make it attainable and may require developing new skills and changing attitudes. The goal is meant to inspire motivation, not discouragement. Think about how to accomplish the goal and if you have the tools/skills needed. If you don't currently possess those tools/ skills, consider what it would take to attain them.

R – **Relevant**- Relevance refers to focusing on something that makes sense with the broader business goals. For example, if the goal is to launch a new product, it should be something that's in alignment with the overall business objectives. Your team may be able to launch a new consumer product, but if your company is a B2B that is not expanding into the consumer market, then the goal wouldn't be relevant.

T – **Time-Bound**- Anyone can set goals, but if it lacks realistic timing, chances are you're not going to succeed. Providing a target date for deliverables is imperative. Ask specific questions about the goal deadline and what can be accomplished within that time period. If the goal will take three months to complete, it's useful to define what should be achieved half-way through the process. Providing time constraints also creates a sense of urgency.

This might feel overwhelming, but not to worry, your *RPI SME* will pretty much do most of this for you, but your goal is to prepare for the T. Time is critical in effective execution. Deadlines, due dates, and schedules are vital to high performers. Or honestly to anyone who gets anything done. Would you have truly ever finished the project, made the slide deck, had the wedding, prepared for the baby, studied for the exam if there was not a due date? I doubt it. Goldfish have such specific goals that being time bound is often not feasible. Goldfish are usually quite rigid with what they are seeking, don't always align with the reality of the marketplace and have a very hard time *pivoting*. That inability usually makes it hard for them to scale. Goldfish do possess the Elephant trait of playing the long game and being willing to wait if needed. However, because these Elephant traits are coupled with the Goldfish traits of rigidity and not understanding the marketplace, they rarely are able to be Elephants. In time, however, acquiring any piece of real estate will always work out financially.

Many Goldfish fall under the assumption that they have to "time the market." In order to consistently "time the market" you generally have to operate full time in real estate—always reading reports and immersing yourself in understanding economic cycles. In other words, you need to build a gut based on experience and reports. For most Goldfish this sort of technical obsession does not exist for them, because it's not their research style. Instead they dial in on one or two indicators which are usually not even very accurate and fail to see the forest through the trees.

TING

Analysis Paralysis Pathway

When we work with our single Goldfish clients, I have noticed we seem to play the role that is typically played by our married client's spouse. If you are a single investor, this is something to be aware of. Indecisiveness, in general, is a Goldfish trait, but for single Goldfish...it can be on steroids.

We met Ting in 2017 and he was starting his pathway to buying his first rental property. I noticed early that he got caught in analysis paralysis, which made his first purchase unsure and insecure. And this prevented him from executing on his second property, even though he was able. If you are able to buy a rental property as a single person, your timing in your younger years can really benefit you and your future family. Who knows, it might even attract the right spouse because she/he sees that you are already focused on building a stable financial foundation for your future family. Remember if you are single you don't *have to* be a Goldfish. Steve the Fox was single and he started his *RPQ* before he got married and started his family.

I've seen our single Goldfish ruminate on worries like:

What if I have a longer vacancy?
What if I don't get the rent that was estimated?
What if property taxes go up too much?
What if the property doesn't appreciate well?
What if the world comes crashing down and everything I worked for goes to hell-in-a-handbasket?"

Yes, these are all real risks, but it's important to remember mantras like:

I will be ok because I play the long game.

Or from Sonny: "I will not lose my peace over anything."

Or from Ben the Top Fox: *"Done is better than perfect."*

Or from Mark Twain: "The secret to getting ahead is getting started..."

Or from Ian: "Accept, Adapt and overcome."

If you still don't know if you are *Willing & Able*, then go back to the first section of this book and refine your *WHY* statement and continue *BANTing* yourself. If you feel like you are unsure, then have a qualified RPI focused real estate agent, property manager or experienced lender qualify you. If you don't know where to find one, then start on the internet. Commit an hour to the web using search terms like *residential property manager, rental property, real estate agent, experienced real estate agent*, and the name of your city, zip code, or area of interest. You will probably find a few people to call.

Ask questions. See who seems helpful and knowledgeable. Someone who is a good fit to assist you in reaching your goals. Repeat this process until you feel you have the right team member to move forward with. This is your first task as a *RPI Business* owner pursuer. This is how it works. Things don't fall in your lap. Especially as a first generation wealth builder, which is very likely what you are if you are a normal person like me. You're going to have to go to work. You are gonna have to find the answers. And then you are going to have to go after what you want. You will have to at least want it for yourself as much as your team members want it for you.

I spent lots of time reminding Ting how to combat his concerns using these techniques. We also reminded him that we use our experience, and history to help predict the future. Once you learn history, then it's pretty much going to work out because history repeats itself. Will it look exactly as you think? No, but what does?

For the single Goldfish investor, it suits them very well to find 'their person' as they go through this process. A mentor, coach, their realtor, or accountability partner are great options. I am still single at the publishing of this book and now that I have my team and processes built, I don't fall back into my Goldfish ways as often. I outsource and trust my qualified team because that is what Elephants do. I also have a mantra that says 'I will work with the best people in the world.' I believe I already am. Feel free to use this mantra or make your own.

Trust me there are still learning curves, even with a team you work with for years or decades. I am having an issue with an HOA on one of my condo rental properties right now and it's quite stressful. Basically, I have a fine of almost $1,000 for bulk items that were set out, allegedly, by my tenant when she moved out. Of course, this should not be my responsibility as the landlord, but it is. The property manager didn't know about this HOA fine until after she itemized and returned the tenant's security deposit so I am stuck holding this bill. I have been arguing this bill with the HOA for the last four months, all the while late fines have been added each month as the dispute continues. They showed me video footage of a person, not my tenant mind you, getting out of a car and putting furniture near the trash dump. You couldn't see the license plate, or the faces of the people who did it. The only thing I could make out is that they were younger people, yet my tenant is in her 70s and just had a stroke. This 'evidence' in no way tied these bulk trash bandits to my property. The HOA doesn't care and to them the video of random people dumping trash is inherently tied to me. Just today I got a letter saying they won't take it off my account and the case is officially closed on their side. Of course, my initial reaction was fury, rage and vengeance. I thought about calling my attorney. Then I played this out after my distressed mind returned to rational sanity and focused on other ways to solve this time-wasting issue.

I brainstormed the pros of my situation:

- I have had the same tenant in this property for all 13 years that I owned it. Thus, I have saved a lot on vacancy, releasing fees and rehabs after tenant move outs. I am still way ahead
- Because this property has never turned over before in my ownership, there were some holes in regard to information on HOA rules. Since I have never had a tenant move out of this complex and neither has my property manager, we are learning a new process together.
- This property has appreciated over 6 times since I bought it. Yes, *over 6 times.* It has been by far my best appreciating property.
- Although the HOA charges ridiculous fines, maybe that is a reason this property has appreciated so much. They run an orderly, well taken care of property and I have benefited in appreciation.
- To allow this expense to not eat my cashflow too aggressively, I can either cut back on other expenses or simply go make more money, because after all…I *am* an entrepreneur.

I can choose to focus on the overwhelming positive benefits of owning this property and redefine this 'fee' as a donation to the Oakhollow Association Beautification Fund. That is how I can categorize it in my mind and feel good about my choice to give. I give generously all year so this will just be one of the organizations I want to support and give to financially this year. Once I went through this process today, my peace was immediately restored. So in review, was it worth me going back and forth with the HOA, debating, having my blood pressure raise, opening letter after letter from them with a new late fee. Having to communicate with them through a mailed or faxed letter rather than by email? I honestly don't think so. Here is the thing, when owning a condo as a rental property, it is a much different animal than a single family. If you don't want an HOA intertwined in your world, then don't buy a condo. Period. I advise every investor I work with not to do so. I got a killer deal on this condo during the *Great Recession* from an old client who wanted out of the business. But this HOA is not fun to deal with compared to my minimally involved single family home HOAs. So as I grow as an investor over the years I will be asking myself is it worth it? One day it might not be, and when that day comes, I will *pivot*.

In a condo, you do not own the land, typically the HOA does. These typically look more like apartments with units above and/or below them, however even properties that DO NOT have other properties above or below them can still be classified as a condo if land ownership does not convey. A condo will almost always have a mandatory HOA, and the HOA will cover common elements including:

TYPICAL ITEMS INCLUDED IN CONDO HOAS:

- Blanket Insurance on the building
- Foundation
- Exterior brick, stone or stucco
- Fence
- Roof
- Sprinkler Systems - both irrigation and fire suppression
- Common Areas
- Reserve accounts
- Some of the utility bills like water, trash, basic cable, valet services, front desk person, security officer, etc.

The good news is that because the HOA dues almost always cover a *Blanket Insurance policy*, this translates into the individual Homeowners Insurance policy costing less because more of the dwelling is covered by the HOA.

The bad news is they are very controlling, have a lot of rules and the high HOA dues almost always kill cashflow. Also if the HOA has an unexpected improvement or large repair they will charge it back to the owners of the association by means of a Special Assessment. Those can be very expensive.

So my goal with this decision was to get out of victim thinking and into *AAO*. *AAO* is the land of milk and honey I assure you. Before Ian taught me about *AAO* and coached me how to get my situations into that process, I often had a hard time making decisions and drove myself into exhaustion with double-mindedness, guilt, being hard on myself and feeling alone and scared (basically living in the Lone Wolf den). So see, even realtors need realtors! I learned this lesson the hard way more than once.

I ended up analyzing dozens of possible properties for Ting, many of which would have worked great. 2017 was a buyers market, so there were plenty of opportunities for him. But it ended up taking him 9 months to pull the trigger and even then he was reluctant. He was always worried the sky was going to fall. If he did solid research, trusted his team, stuck to the *4-in-10*, it would have all worked out. After all he was on track to buy property #2 before COVID, but he just kept getting cold feet. If he bought anything in 2019 or 2020 after COVID, he would have had excellent returns! He did end up refinancing in Dec 2020 when rates were at 40 year lows, similar to Ben, so that was a huge win for him!

Let's take a look at Ting's *RPQ* of 1:

Property Name & Details	Prop #1 - 4/3/2 SFH built in 2016 with 2400 Sq Ft
Year Bought	Apr 2018
Purchase Price	$285,000
Down Payment (DP) %	25%
Total Cash to Close (DP = Closing Costs (CC)	$69,100
2025 Value	$359,400
Total Years Owned	7.5
$ Total Equity Gain (2015 Value when She sold to me)	$74,400
% Total Equity Gain	26%
% Equity Gain - Annulized	3.48%
ROI (Total Equity / Total Cash to Close	107.67%
ROI (Total Equity / Total Cash to Close -Annualized Return	14.36%

DON'T BE A CAUTIONARY *'TAIL'*

Have you noticed you have been swimming and swimming yet going nowhere? Is it possible that you are a Goldfish? Let's recap the Goldfish traits to see:

They...

- Can't clearly define their criteria, due to lack of proper research techniques
- Value their feelings more than facts
- May be labeled by others as *illogical*
- Are usually idealistic
- Make a great friend, but maybe not a great client

- Are fear based because they don't do adequate research before they get started, which turns into analysis paralysis
- Decide the plan and tell the leader vs. the other way around
- Are very loyal and kind
- Take a long time to make a decision
- Are good at starting, but not great at finishing
- Can have people pleasing tendencies
- Don't trust the process

Goldfish get caught in the past or the future, and they have a hard time staying in the *big picture present* like Elephants and Foxes do. There is a defensive passivity that has to be shed for Goldfish to realize their potential, swim against the tide, and transform into their full potential.

Goldfish have a short term memory about what they agreed to, because as time goes on they follow their feelings and feelings can change a lot. And because there is a lack of trusting the plan and process, their feelings are their dominant compass. They have a vision, but it's so narrow, niche and possibly unrealistic it is easy for them and their team to get burnt out along the way and not *execute* it practically. In other words, they want to reinvent the wheel because sometimes their vision is so strong.

Due to lack of research, Goldfish typically can't clearly define their criteria. When they do, they use ambiguous statements like 'I want a good cash flow' and 'I want the tenant to lease quickly and for a long time' and 'I don't want a lot of expenses to prepare the property for the initial tenant.' What does 'good, quickly, long and a lot' mean? It's ok to not know how to answer these questions as a new RPI, but it's much more effective when you ask these as questions as opposed to making statements. In other words, 'what range should I expect for cash flow? What is the estimated time of vacancy in this area and how should I best prepare for it financially? What is the average time a tenant stays in this type of rental in this area? Is it possible that my Buy Box Criteria will allow me more of a turn key rental to keep initial costs low?' How would a first time RPI even know to ask these questions? Because they did their research. In other words, research helps them learn the right questions to ask. Goldfish forget this principle. Don't forget this principle.

I would encourage you to beware of Goldfish tendencies. Be willing to flex with the market and *pivot* your plan, separating yourself from emotion. Indecision *is* a decision. It's a choice to delay, cause fatigue, and ultimately to miss out. Tell me dear friend, what is it you plan to do with your one wild and precious life? I can't imagine you wanting to be a Goldfish your whole life now that you know how big the ocean is. Don't you want to get out of that bowl and really go for a swim? I am sure glad I did. Goldfish-Lone Wolf hybrids can become Elephants. How do I know? Because that is my story and my pathway is up next dear friend.

CHAPTER THIRTEEN

My Elephant Pathway

How do you eat an Elephant? One bite at a time.
In other words it won't happen overnight. That is the #1 characteristic our Elephants have in reaching their financial and investing goals. They all played the long game.

Quick Description: An Elephant is a self-made millionaire having 1 million dollars or more in rental property portfolio net worth. You can do that with only 4 properties within a couple of decades. Elephants understand it's imperative to have a great attitude by seeing whatever happens in their journey as a lesson vs a sabotage. They do not let comparison get in their head. They understand it is their independent race and they are the only competitor in it. They have an internal compass shaped by their mission and visi=on, years of experience, trial and error, and lessons.

Elephants are usually the mentors that normal people like you and me have always looked for as we began our journey as investors. They are the real life, attainable, humble, below the radar, arms-length regional success stories that you can emulate to build your own success. If you don't have any actual Elephant mentors in your life yet, please borrow ours. Another key ingredient of Elephants is that they pay it forward and value teaching the next generation, because at some point on their great migration, someone taught them.

What does *success* look like to you?

I have pried into this question for many years. I once stumbled on a YouTube video called *Your Dream Life List* that helped me get to the bottom of this question. The challenge was to create a list of everything that would constitute a personalized version of a dream life. The instructions clearly stated that in your dream life absolutely nothing was off limits, it could be whatever you wanted. I made the list and quickly learned that everything I truly wanted was actually attainable. But how could that be?

Let me encourage you to make a list. Search your heart, be truthful, carve out a private moment and make a list, your list. If you already have one, take an audit of it or draft a new one—even right now, whether it's in the margins of this book or on scrap paper. What does your list consist of? Maybe it includes being a loving husband or wife. Perhaps you want a fruitful relationship with your children or grandchildren and for your family to be healthy and happy. Maybe you want to travel to exciting places like to see the Northern Lights in Norway or the Galapagos Islands. Reach millionaire status maybe? Do you want to reach *financial freedom* or pay for your child's college to anywhere they want to go, start a business, or buy a home on a beach?

Without peeking at your list, I am willing to bet that you did not list the desire to be the King of Saudi Arabia or to become the first person on Mars, did you? You likely did not write that your dream was to run a two-minute-mile or to buy Mount Everest. If you are like most, *Your Dream Life List* includes a beautiful life, your perfect life and ultimately things that are actually, truly attainable. Like really doable. Some of the highlights on my list included desiring to be a good wife and good mother, owning a Labradoodle, helping to train up the next generation of RPIs, having discipline in working out regularly and eating for health and vitality—thus living in my right size body, doing more of the work I want to do and less of the work I don't want to do, and owning a beach house. All very, very attainable. Wouldn't you agree? Some of these I could literally attain today or start the beginning steps toward them.

Like owning a Labradoodle (I could literally buy one today or start the adoption process today). Owning a beach house (I could literally afford to buy one today if I wanted to). Although I couldn't afford a beach house in Malibu, I'll bet there is a beach house somewhere that I could afford. Now maybe I am not truly willing to do either of these two things today, which is why I have not done them yet. I think the timing is just off on both, but the fact is I could if I chose to. I am *able*. But honestly, maybe I am not willing. Once *Willing & Able* intersect for me, then they will be accomplished.

I bet your results would be the same. You will find things on your list that you are able, but not willing, or willing, but not able, or perhaps neither. Perhaps after this exercise, you will decide to *execute* some things that are within your reach now. And maybe some things on your list you might never realize. But it might not be because you were not able. Maybe in the depth of your honesty, you might discover you are not *Willing & Able*. Maybe they are old dreams or passing dreams you latched onto, or perhaps someone else's dreams. Regardless, if you decide to actually pursue all of your dream life or not, you will find that pretty much everything on your list is attainable. Once you acknowledge that, then you need to believe it, so you can start your pursuit of achieving your dream life. It's actually that simple. And what else have you got to do anyway? This could be a moment for you. The moment where you realize that your dream life is actually possible. Maybe your friends or family won't see it like this or agree, but that is not what you are going to focus on. If they are not reading this book and updating their narrative with the language of our community, then how could they fully understand how you think now? I believe in you. The Elephants you will soon read about believe in you. How do I fully know you are capable? Because, you are the only one on earth that is qualified to be you. Past, present and future. There will never be another you. Ever. These dreams of your heart were not placed there willy-nilly. These dreams are your destiny, you were precisely crafted and woven together in your mother's womb, made for a calling and purpose. You live on earth at this exact time in history and technology and are capable of accomplishing way more than you could truly fathom. Your valuable, precious, miraculous life has infinite possibilities of success and outcome. You have a choice in how you succeed. No one, I mean no one, gets a weighted opinion on the matter unless it's to help you reach your dream life. We have plenty of people telling us we can't, don't we? Let's revel in the patriarchs and matriarchs of our little animal investor kingdom for a bit and receive these Elephants who will tell you, you can. Put yourself in their story. You can repeat what they did, because their pathways won't be going out of style. RPI will never go away. Ever. The reason is because there will always be owners and always be renters. Even when we get to Mars and start colonizing.

THE AMERICAN DREAM IS YOURS FOR THE TAKING...SO TAKE IT.

Even before I knew all of my dream life heart's desires, I vowed to build a better life at 16 than the one I came from, and I have done so. I will continue to do so. I'm going after what is available to me. America and the promise of her dream have afforded me and other Elephants a greenhouse in which we can grow and flourish. And it's anyone's for the taking, so take it. Claim your inheritance of the *American Dream*!

I have been to 24 countries so far for personal travel, some of which I have been to two or three times. Which, by the way, almost all of this travel was done very frugally and before I *became*. Some advanced like Great Britain, Australia, Singapore, Switzerland and most of Europe, Dubai, Taiwan and Japan. Some were third world and developing countries like the Dominican Republic, Morocco, Argentina, Panama, Puerto Rico, Mexico and most recently Kenya, Africa. Every time I come back home I am beyond grateful to pull that American Passport out of my backpack and walk toward the line that says US Citizens. While it is not Utopia, it is a land of opportunity where economic mobility is available unlike anywhere on earth. This is evidenced by the fact that the USA takes in more immigrants annually than every other nation of the world combined. Untraveled Americans can take America for granted. It's hard to fully understand how valuable and full of opportunity this place is, when you haven't seen, smelled, tasted, felt, and heard how the others around the world live. And there are way more of the others than there are Americans in this huge world. Americans only make up 4% of the world's population. You heard that right, 96% of the people on earth don't live here. It's no coincidence that many people want US citizenship. Poet Ralph Waldo Emerson declared, "America is another name for opportunity." It was true then, it is true today and it will be true tomorrow. I have brought up America the Beautiful several times in this book. I have done it purposefully because we live in a cynical world. And a cynical America. Have you noticed that many of these cynical Americans have never spent real time out of America? Additionally have you noticed that cynical Americans are not in the 7% millionaire club? I have found that for all of the Elephant pathways in this book as well as many others I didn't write about, the theme is that America does indeed offer opportunity. I asked each Elephant if they think the *American Dream* is still alive and well today in their interviews and if someone today could do what they did. All of them said heck yes. So if all of them said yes, then that means the *American Dream* is still alive. So be careful who you take your advice from when it comes to building wealth. I would challenge you against taking advice from someone about wealth building, when they themselves don't have wealth.

I, like other Elephants, made a decision. I wasn't going to let cynicism take me off track from where I decided I was going. I would not let any political climate or party platform interfere with my goals. I wasn't going to let all the people who say I can't or won't be successful interfere. I wasn't going to get caught up in other people's dreams and ideas thus losing my own. I wasn't going to miss my destiny. No. Matter. What. If it was possible, and I KNEW it was possible in America, then I would indeed pursue my dream. So I pursued it and didn't give up until I reached my own proverbial Ellis Island.

If you choose to stay in America, then make that choice and take off the cloak of cynicism. Put on the cloak of gratitude in the system that is available to you and play the game. There are probably quintillions of dollars out there to be claimed because money is more or less infinite. You just need to claim your own inheritance of it if you are *Willing & Able.* You probably just need to know *how.*

The main thing I always got caught up on in my pursuit was *the how.* I always knew what I wanted to invest in, why I wanted to invest in it, but I never really understood *the how.* This is your window into *the how.*

HEATHER

My Becoming an Elephant migration story

Being an Elephant means you have financial freedom and you focus on being *balance sheet rich.* I learned about this concept over the Pacific Ocean heading to Australia in 2011. I was slowly reading the first book I read as a professional called *The Millionaire Mind,* by

Thomas J. Stanley (the same author who wrote The *Millionaire Next Door* that helped shape Sarah the Fox's investor mind). This book was not an easy read because it was so data heavy and it ended up taking me about 2 years of off-and-on reading to finish. But even then, I had an Elephant core value peaking out which was that I finish what I start. Dr. Stanley wrote that the first generation millionaires they surveyed and studied focused on their *balance sheet* (assets minus liabilities) more than their *income statement* (income minus expenses). Of course these two financial reports and the understanding of them have to work in symbiosis, but my rudimentary takeaway was to focus on building assets and the rest would work out. In a nut shell, play the long game. Simply put, an *asset* is something that increases in value over time and the value is stored on your *balance sheet*. RPI is all about becoming *balance sheet rich*. Eventually those *assets* like rental property will generate income like an annuity or pension. I adopted the ideology that I really like knowing I could buy anything I wanted in cash, but probably never would. I liked that power, that freedom of never worrying about money in the future. Remember it's not what you make it's what you keep. In other words if you make $10,000,000 a year and spend $10,000,000 on non-asset garbage, you are broke. Being an Elephant is about the process of building. If you live like a pauper for a little while, you can live like a king or queen forever. That is a kingdom mindset.

All of our Elephants are first generation millionaires and therefore almost all of these Elephants have a background of time served in other animal categories on their way to *becoming*. I never planned to be a Lone Wolf, and in my deepest state of Lone Wolf-ness I didn't really even recognize it. I never thought I was controlling, egotistical, prideful, even mean at times. But I had some of those *moments*. I wasn't typically the kind that would go for your jugular, but I would put you on my score card and hold a grudge. If I lost a deal, I would just work twice as hard to make it up, which fueled into workaholism, which as you know almost took me out. All of that was rooted in me being a Lone Wolf. I honestly didn't know another way and didn't have a clear idea of how to get where I wanted to go in a more peaceful way. I grew up with scripted soap operas as my guide. I thought life was supposed to have drama, extreme highs and lows, and a winner and a loser. I knew in my heart there was a better life in the Fox hole or on the Elephant migration trail and I yearned to get there.

I also had no intention of swimming around in a small Goldfish tank, but those shortsighted tendencies did manifest a time or two, or perhaps 800 times. I had to learn how to have boundaries, how to separate my feelings, how to build and thrive in consistent processes and systems, how to do proper research, how to not act on my *entrepreneurial seizures* as Michael E. Gerber from *The-Myth Revisited* calls them, for days, weeks, months, and even years. I had to *pivot* from consciously incompetent to unconsciously competent and define what I was doing, who I was doing it for, when I was going to do it, where I was doing it, why I was doing it in the first place and how I was going to do it.

These days I am more aligned with the Elephant than ever, but it did not happen overnight. My whole life I have been internally driven to find the right people because I was always searching for who I wanted to be. I was searching for my role models. In 2023, I reached year 20 in my *10-10-10 Career Plan* (mentioned in the introduction) and I knew I needed an *SME* to help build my next company which would teach the next generation how to RPI. *Rental Property U (RPU)* was born, although it didn't officially get incorporated until a year later in 2024 (just like in Ben's story). I then started looking for that *SME* and I found Michael, a business coach, who became a role model for me. Because Michael had a vast experience in building and running scalable businesses, he qualified me and after discerning I was

Willing & Able, he helped me *pick a pathway* to get started. We decided on the pathway of making a RPI e-course and then to start writing this very book. Then, he connected me with his independent publisher and editor Nick, the *SME* in his space, who helped him write his own book, *Next Level Life*. Nick helped build my confidence even more, gave me a key lesson in how to be a first time author which was to sit down every day for 30 minutes a day with the phone on the other side of the room and to simply...write. No less than 30 minutes a day. If I missed a day, then do 1 hour the next day. If I missed 3 days, then do 1.5 hours. But don't go more than missing 3 days. Nick also helped me shape my book idea by creating this very outline for me and I began filling it in. About the same time, I started working with a marketing coach Joe (who is also an Airbnb investor) to help me come up with the investor animals concept. I originally showed up with a concept that included 22 RPI pathways that I wanted to name and thought people could remember sort of modeled after a book I had read called *Strengthsfinder 2.0* and he, very wisely, advised me to narrow them down to 4. He said no one is going to remember all the pathways you want them to and said name 22 shampoo brands. After I couldn't get past 4, the point was made. With our magic number of 4 in mind, Ian and I came up with the animal concept once we realized that our investors truly did fit into 4 categories and the animal names just sort of easily came out once we identified that.

After I started writing and when I would have trouble believing that little ole' me could be an author, my friend from church Cheryl reminded me that the untrained writers wrote the best selling book of all time, The Holy Bible. Then as I wrote and re-wrote and re-wrote again and another long time *SME* coach that I have, Katherine would remind me of my goals of why I wanted to do this in the first place when I forgot or got discouraged (which was alot). And then I was lucky enough to have Ian who was continuously positive without ceasing, abundantly encouraging, and truly believed I could do it. How many times did he spend during our team meetings building me up and standing firm in the truth that I could indeed be a published author in a topic that I understood and was qualified to teach. I also had a new investor I met in Colorado before I started to write the 4th edit named Deb that I named as 'the one' I was writing this book for. The normal, first time RPI who was a lot like Ben before he got started. When I got lost in my mission, I reminded myself I am just writing this book for one person. That person is Deb. Then my Aunt Karen was rooting me on, along with most of the people I wrote about in this book. And of course all the dream cheerleaders behind the scenes including, but not limited to, my dear friends Amanda, Pei Wen, Sivi, Vanessa, Ferlina, John, Cheryl L, Eugene, Josh, Jacque, Hailey, Robert, Shelley, David M, Amy, another Deb, Julie, Julia, Haley, Lydia, Tonnie, Abigail, Rosalyn, Samantha, Mitzi, Barbie, Sydney, Lyann, Christian, Martha, Heather L, Brianna, Nicole, Julio, David E, Jackie, David D, Johnny, Lisa, Hudson, Jack, Tony, Leng, Molly, Broc, Maria, Katherine G, Stacey, Pilar, Sarah N, Pastor Jenn, Christy & my sisters Tiffany and Leigh Ann. And then when I was struggling to get the 6th edit done, what I thought would be my last...my dear friend Michelle saw the draft hard copy sitting on my desk and also saw my statement on my vision board that said 'Published 2025 first Time Author' next to a print out image of the initial book cover art mock up and she said, "can I read it and give you feedback?" I couldn't believe she would do that. But not only did she say she would do it, she actually did. And then gave me incredible feedback which led to a much improved 7th edit and the reason for the *grey boxes*. This was the longest singularly focused project I have ever completed, which from start to publish took 2 1/2 years and 10 edits. I thought it was kind of a neat coincidence that the time frame an Elephant is pregnant is also about 2 years?

Without every single one of these people in my corner, I can attest to the absolute fact that I would have never, ever, ever completed this book. I don't know much, but I know this about myself. I cannot do big projects like this on my own. Elephants tend to know this truth also. They know that you can't do big things alone, nor would they want to. I recall hearing an interview with Warren Buffet and he said that he could run his firm alone without Charlie Munger, sure, but "it just wouldn't be that much fun." After all, isn't a happy life all about sharing it with friends, family, community...and having fun? As a Lone Wolf, it's pretty hard to have fun, enjoy the process and celebrate victories. As an Elephant I know without a doubt if you don't, you are missing the entire point of *becoming*. It truly is about the migration and not the destination. Because the Elephant migration is your whole life. So you might as well enjoy it, right?

So in your pursuit, the right people are always the most important ingredient. Money comes second. And honestly the hidden 'secret' is that money always follows good relationships. Elephants understand this law of success. Elephants understand that in the end it's really not the one with the most toys who wins, because they know they can't take it with them. It's more about how you treat people along the way and what you stewarded. That is your real legacy.

Every self-help book typically has a format of I did it the wrong way, then I learned the right way, here is what I learned and now you can skip all the pain and do it the right way. However, this lightning in a bottle solution is not fully true because sometimes you will touch the hot stove by accident at the very least. Why? Because you simply don't know what you don't know...and all us are still learning as we go. No one on earth has lived tomorrow right? Today is the dress rehearsal and final act all in one show. So read this guide book, reread it, use it as a resource, but give yourself a lot of grace, love, and peace.

As your loving RPI Elephant matriarch, I dearly want you to be successful and happy. And I truly believe you can do both.

I didn't give you much information about my upbringing in the introduction, but just know it was probably similar to many peoples. It was hard. Very hard. But aren't all of our lives at some point and to some degree? It's not where you are going, it's where you end. And like every one's parents, mine made sacrifices and so did yours. For their sacrifices I am genuinely grateful. My life progress and success was in no way straight up and to the right, and if you are a first generation millionaire, yours will not be either. But because I got started and I never gave up on my mission, I got there. And you will too, if you follow that formula.

So enough about my past, let's talk about your bright future so you can get started on building your own *RPQ*. You can use my pathway or any of the investors you like or pathwork your own. Here are the details of my *RPQ*. Due to the fact that I know every single detail about my own portfolio, I thought it would be valuable to show you the truth in extreme detail and did my best to encapsulate that best I could with that soft science caveat I mentioned in the beginning disclaimer.

Property Name & Details	Prop #1 Condo - 1/1.5, Detached . Garage built in 2003 with 960 sq ft	Prop #2 - 50% Co-owned with LT Boyfriend* 4/4/2, built in 2002 with 3854 sq ft	Prop #3 Condo- 3/2 no garage built in 1981 with 1200 sq ft	Prop #4 - Small Apartment Building #1 - I own 25%* - Co-Owned with 75% Business Partner -15 Units - 13 2/2 & 2 1/1 - Built in 1960, renovated in 2021	Prop #5 - Small Apartment Building #2 - I own 25%* - Co-Owned with 75% Business Partner -21 Units All 1/1 - Built in 1985
Year Bought	Dec 2006	Mar 2008	Oct 2012	Jan 2013	Jan 2013
Purchase Price	$165,000	$307,900	$25,881	$420,000	$810,000
Down Payment (DP) %	0%	5%**	100%	0%**	5%**
Total Cash to Close (DP = Closing Costs (CC)	$2,500	$17,115	$26,850	$2,833	$44,370
Year Sold	Feb 2020	Aug 2014			
Price Sold	$221,000	$377,000			
Rehab Amount	$12,853	$5,000***	$5,000*	$1,470,000***	$1,300,000***
2025 Value	$268,300	$672,500	$170,800	$2,200,000	$2,400,000
Total Years Owned	13.25	5.5	13	12.75	12.75
$ Total Equity Gain - Rehab Amount - Ok this is where it is going to get complicated I will use 50% and 25% calculations to show my portion	$43,147	$48,414	$139,919	$182,500	$275,000
% Total Equity Gain	26%	16%	541%	43%	34%

% Equity Gain - Annulized	1.97%	2.86%	41.59%	3.41%	2.66%
ROI (Total Equity / Total Cash to Close	1725.88%	282.87%	521.11%	6441.93%	619.79%
ROI (Total Equity / Total Cash to Close -Annualized Return	130.26%	51.43%	40.09%	505.25%	48.61%
Notes*	Did 80/20 Loan, 0% down and rolled in most closing costs	*Not Recommended to buy property with boyfriends or girlfriends. I am using the whole value but note I only owned 50%	*Same Section 8 tenant from 2006 - 2025. Only did repainting and light $4,000 rehab at 2025 move out	*I am recording the full amounts, but Note I only own 25%	*I am recording the full amounts, but Note I only own 25%
Notes**		**Even though we were 50/50 owners, the agreement was that he would be the only one on the Loan and I would put the 5% down payment down. I would get this paid back when we sold in 2014 before we split profit.		**Bought for 420k with a 1-year Wrap Loan Seller Financing option. We assumed Seller's Note at 390k so brought $36,534 to closing. I was the Realtor along with my commercial realtor partner Gary so we split commissions of $12,600. I used my Realtor commissions toward my 25% down payment equal to $9,133.50 and therefore had to only bring $2,833 to closing.	**Total Down payment was 20% and total cash to close was $177,480. My portion of that was 25% and my business partner contributed 75%.

Notes ***		*** Make ready to sell was $5,000 but my portion was $2,500		*** We did 2 cash-out refinances to finance the Renovation that cost about $1.6 Million. It was a huge renovation during COVID from 2020-2022. That is an entire other book.	*** We took out 2 cash-out refinances to renovate 1 unit and the exterior of the building. We overbid on our other apartment's full renovation so that we had to use equity from this building to cover all the mis-calculations.

Props 6-11

Property Name & Details	Prop #6 - Bought for displaced* Section 8 Tenant - 3/2.5/2 SFH built in 2000 with 3278 Sq Ft	Prop #7 - BRRR Strategy - 3/2.5/2 SFH built in 1998 with 1470 Sq Ft	Prop #8 Prop I bought from Dee- 3/2.5/2 Townhome built in 2007 with 1939 Sq Ft	Prop #9 - 4/2.5/2 SFH built in 2002 with 2354 Sq Ft	Prop #10 Attempted BRRR- SFH - 2/1 with 1 car detached garage built in 1945 with 1085 Sq Ft	Prop #11 - My current House - Renovated Move-Up -3/3/2.5 with a pool built in 1980 with 2660 Sq Ft
Year Bought	Nov 2013	June 2014	July 2015	Dec 2015	Dec 2017	Nov 2024
Purchase Price	$141,000	$138,000	$235,000	$210,000	$140,000	$450,000
Down Payment (DP) %	25%	18%	20%	25%	0%*	33%
Total Cash to Close (DP = Closing Costs (CC)	$41,357	$21,585	$37,421	$55,528	$1,690	$150,307
Year Sold	Jul 2020				July 2020	
Price Sold	$250,000				$249,990	
Rehab Amount	$34,863	$15,000*	$0	$28,000	$53,380**	$133,217*

2025 Value	$330,660	$299,600	$383,000	$369,400	$298,500	$550,000**
Total Years Owned	6.5	11.5	10.5	10	2.5	1
$ Total Equity Gain - Rehab Amount	$74,137	$161,600	$148,000	$159,400	$56,610	-$33,217
% Total Equity Gain	53%	117%	63%	76%	40%	-7%
% Equity Gain -Annulized	8.09%	10.18%	6.00%	7.59%	16.17%	-7.38%
ROI (Total Equity / Total Cash to Close	179.26%	748.67%	395.50%	287.06%	3349.70%	-22.10%
ROI (Total Equity / Total Cash to Close -Annualized Return	27.58%	65.10%	37.67%	28.71%	1339.88%	-22.10%
Notes*	*I don't recommend buying a property for a tenant who asks you to do so because you feel bad for them. Buy them a meal, not a house.			*Bought this at night using a flashlight. I also don't recommend this.	*I did private financing from Khai who owns his mortgage brokerage. It was a 5 year loan at 4% amortized over 20 years with a balloon for the remaining amount.	*I initially budgeted $60,000, which quickly changed to $90,000 and ended up at $132,000. I built a traditional Finnish Sauna, ripped out and rebuilt the entire master bathroom, added electrical sockets everywhere I wanted them and ordered custom kitchen cabinet & drawer pull outs, as well as bought a $2,000 life size horse lamp because I got out of control. But I also, for the first time in all of my house buying days, got what I wanted. The rehab took 3.5 months and I moved in March 1, 2025.

Notes**					**I did an initial rehab of $39,047 before I moved in which included an unexpected $6,000 plumbing line replacement. I didn't do a Plumbing Static Pressure Test for $295 and I paid the price. I did the remaining exterior landscaping, fence addition & deck rehab before I sold in 2020 for an extra $14,000.	**It's hard to say what it's worth because I essentially built a custom home in a neighborhood that has lots of renovated houses and comps, but it might come in short if I sold today because we are in a flat to declining market in 2025-2026.

So as you can see I made some buys, some sells, and had some unexpected situations. That is how the game is played, though for us first generation folk and I would argue many of the Blue Whales, there will be lots of unexpected twists and turns in your migration that you could have never guessed until they occur.

The secret to getting ahead is getting started, so even with all the mistakes and misfortune I had along the way, I am still standing and all is well. Don't forget, you must keep playing the game. If I gave up on edit 3, trust me, you would never be reading this book right now and I would be saying what-if still in 2045. I would have never known what could have been and that would be very painful. Everyone on their deathbed has those types of regrets and I simply didn't want to. So I did whatever I needed to do to keep going and get to the execution line which in this book writing world is called publishing. Is it scary? YES. It's a vulnerable place to translate your thoughts into a written and bound book that strangers will read and criticise. We all know the critique's can be the loudest voices we hear. But I am ok with whatever comes, but I know in my soul I have to do this. However, I believe that what will come will be wonderful and therefore, no matter what it is, it will be. I have been preparing to write this book for 23 years. I made a decision to write it. And I wrote it. There is no other expectation I am placing on it other than to publish it. But deep down I know that this book will unlock a new path for my bright future. And RPI will do the same for you. I just know it. I know it like I know that rocks are hard and water is wet.

You can lock in that truth dear friend. I am the *RPI SME* that you hired by buying this book to tell you the truth. I know the truth because I have analyzed 1000's of rental properties over 2 decades. Real estate always always always goes up. It is just a function of time. If you commit to playing the long game, if you are *Willing & Able*, you cannot lose. Think of a world where the word lose does not exist. That is this world. It is yours for the taking. Not everyone will take it. Will you?

Elephants play this long game of monopoly. And sometimes the best path forward is not buying *Park Place*. For most Elephants, they differ from Foxes in that they have very low to non-existent, paid off mortgages by this point. Elephants have impressive *balance sheets* and a healthy financial perspective. They know their goals, say no to things that don't align, play well on teams, and they know they will get where they are going....eventually.

No one knows the future, but many times we let fear or short term judgment make our decisions. That is what happened to me when my Goldfish syndrome showed up just a short while ago during COVID. I wish I had someone like me to talk me out of selling the three rental properties I sold because I let fear creep in because it's a fact that you can't be your own counselor, open heart surgeon or divorce attorney. That is why we need a good team around us.

CHAPTER FOURTEEN

Are You the Elephant?

With at least $1 million in rental property assets over a couple of decades, things are very likely going to work out for you and your family, wouldn't you agree? That was my train of thought and mission anyway, and let me tell you it did work out like that. Just try it, all the cool Elephants are doing it. RPI is the new black. Working toward your financial freedom has been ranked the most attractive millionaire next door quality by the best selling *Becoming an Elephant book club*. Come on friend, join our club. If you have a strong *why* and think you are at the intersection of *Willing & Able*, just start with your first rental property. It's the reason why I wrote this book—not just to give you more information, but to help you qualify yourself. And if you are *Willing & Able*, then my goal has been to show you how normal people like you and me did it so you can *Pick Your Pathway* and get started, because the secret to getting ahead is getting started.

And remember, there is nothing to be scared of because you are just *picking your V1 pathway*, you will very likely change pathways as you grow through your life. Choose one, and follow the pathway of these real life RPI pathways so you can *execute*. That is the way new investors eventually became Elephants. Remember, every pathway in this book is about normal people like you and me who got started because they were *Willing & Able*. I hope I have drilled it into you by now that getting started and not giving up until you reach your vision is more valuable than any other factor. The micro or macro market conditions, the interest rates, the political party currently in power, the sensationalism of speculatory news headlines, the fear of AI taking over the world, whatever Wall Street is saying or not saying, the trends, the cynical world we live in reminding you how hard and risky this path will be do not hold a candle to the time value of money which is the peanut butter to the jelly of Mark Twain's always relevant advice: "The secret to getting ahead is (and everybody now...) getting started."

It took me a long time to find the mentor I'm trying to be for you. For years, I drove to work feeling imposter syndrome, having to do power stances in my car or bathroom mirror before leading team meetings. I watched YouTube videos on firing someone just minutes before doing it. Seeing billboards of companies like Hilton or Starbucks depressed me because I felt so far from achieving that level of success.

RPI was the only thing I truly understood. It seemed truly attainable for normal people like me. Sure it takes work and time, but doesn't everything that matters in life? Remember, there's a 99% chance of getting rich slowly and only a 1% chance of getting rich quickly.

Remember, the Statista.com data from the introduction? There are only 7% of Americans, or 23.83 million Americans who are millionaires as of the end of 2024.[9]

9. Statista. "The Number of Millionaires Keeps Rising (Chart: The Number of Dollar Millionaires [in Millions] in Selected Countries in 2000, 2024 and Forecast for 2028)." *Statista*, September 4 2025. Accessed November 18 2025. https://www.statista.com/chart/30671/number-of-millionaires-and-share-of-the-population/?srsltid=AfmBOoos9jQvcLgvuTsHkcpp3Fd4vZKaR-yepcZNBMVyuqDLxSIHuh8-. Statista

As you read the following Elephant pathways, you might find that you are *Willing & Able* to pursue a portion of their pathway. Many of these Elephants have longer, diverse, multi-migrated pathways within their pathway. Break them up, cut and paste, design your *Version 1* migration however you like. Whatever it takes for you to get started, because the secret to getting ahead is getting started. Every investment vertical and pathway works for at least one person, but not every investment vertical and pathway works for everyone. You will have to discern what your investment vertical is now. Remember the more successful you become, the more offers you will receive. Knowing your why and having a plan will help you stay on your course to the 7% club.

There are even investment vertices within investment vertices. For example in the whole overarching category of Real Estate Investing, there are two subcategories called *Residential* and *Commercial*. Beyond this, there are even more subcategory niche pathways to choose from. You will read about some of these asset types in the Elephant pathways to follow.

MAIN RESIDENTIAL & COMMERCIAL REAL ESTATE INVESTMENT VERTICALS & ASSET TYPES:

RESIDENTIAL:

- Single Family Homes (SFH)
- Condos
- Townhomes
- Duplex
- Triplex
- Quadruplex
- Manufactured homes
- New Construction
- Micro Homes and Tiny Homes
- Mobile Homes

- Rental Property
- Flips
- Wholesales
- Cosale
- Buy, Rehab, Rent, Refinance (BRRR)
- Subject-to
- Seller Financing

COMMERCIAL:

- Small Apartment Buildings
- Large Apartment Buildings
- Office Buildings
- Industrial and Warehouses
- Land Leases
- Strip Malls or Shopping Malls - Retail
- Oil and Gas
- Farm and Ranch - i.e. Raw Land
- Subdivision Development
- Hospitals
- Resorts
- Hotels
- Mixed-Use Development
- Manufacturing
- Special Purpose

For our Elephant pathways, we are going to take a deeper look into their investing portfolios, different from our other animals, because they have more to report on. Since Elephants are our north star and have reached what we call success, I would like to invite you to a kitchen table discussion of their specific journey. When did they buy, sell, how much did they spend, invest, lose, gain. Where did they come from and what do they do now? How long did it take them and what did they learn? Take what you like and l, leave the rest. You already have more information in reading this one guidebook than I and almost all of these Elephant investors did when they started. The only pressure you might feel when reading their decades-in-the-making stories is what you put on yourself. And why in the world would you want to treat your precious self like that? So, relax in that fact and enjoy my dear friends.

AUNT KAREN AND UNCLE FREDDY

Land Pathway

Though I observed them at a distance growing up, my Aunt Karen and Uncle Freddy were my earliest role models of success in entrepreneurship and in real estate. I only saw them once every couple of months growing up, but they were very successful and I took note of that early. Even families of humble beginnings often have that one outlier of success that can be admired and duplicated. They were the ones who broke out and "made it."

"Land is a good investment because they are not making more of it," my Aunt Karen would say. She picks up on things others don't as clearly. For example, she recognized early in my life that I needed to be in sales. She saw me winning sales contests at The Gap when I was 16 and pursuing their coveted Gold Badge program by 18 and knew sales was a field I would thrive in. She was the only one in my life that highlighted my strong attributes to me. As I grew up, she later pinpointed that I should be in Real Estate. That was a *moment* for me—and she was right on both. She never knew what an influence on my early life she really made, as well as when I grew up and became a real estate investor. She and my Uncle Freddy were the ones that did it successfully and showed me it was possible. I would end up gleaning on their Elephant blueprint my entire life.

They always played the long game when it came to the land investments and small business they built. They would buy something that was on the outskirts of town knowing that in time it would develop. Their biggest attribute, being land investors, was their ability to hold. Patience is indeed a virtue, yet it is rare in this pervasive and loud instantly gratified culture. Elephants have embedded patience for their long journey.

My Aunt grew up with my mother and two other sisters in a two bedroom shack on an 88 acre farm in the middle of the woods about 50 miles south of Fort Worth, TX in the 1940s-1950's. They had no running water or indoor plumbing. They were very poor. Over the years due to the land's deep country location, it was not worth very much more than a few hundred bucks an acre. But since 2000, 50 years later, when DFW started to sprawl, it has gone up to several thousand an acre. The history lesson here is that all land rises in value, but the x factor is time. Hold it long enough and it will always increase in value.

My grandpa passed away in 2017 and willed a 1/3 of it to her. Aunt Karen bought out Aunt Linda's 1/3 and then gifted it to the youngest Aunt Gayle who now owns the full 88 acres. What a gift that was! My mom, the 4th sister, inherited the house in town that my grandparents bought in 1975, which was worth about $115,000 in 2017 because my mom didn't want the land. So now Aunt Gayle is on her way to generational wealth as a land owner like Aunt Karen. That makes two of the four sisters millionaires, due to their land holdings.

The earlier history of this 88 acres was that it was initially bought by my great grandmother Momo in the early 1900s who borrowed money from her sister. Momo was very poor too and paid the loan back by selling chickens. Unfortunately the chicken payment plan caused a rift with her sister and a disagreement over money, as the story commonly goes, that lasted several decades. It is resolved now so *amen,* but time was lost. Momo knew, like Aunt Karen, Aunt Gayle and my grandpa that land is always valuable. One piece of land can change a generation, and it has.

Would you like to be the Momo or the grandpa or the Aunt Karen and Uncle Freddy of your own generational downline? Momo or grandpa never got to see what this land will do for our family, but I will. It will change Aunt Gayle's three daughters and their children's lives and so on. Would you be willing to 'sell chickens' to pursue a legacy of setting up your generational downline for possible generations to come? Momo had a calling for this land. She had vision beyond herself. She got creative, risked a family relationship, held it decades without seeing the value rise, and played the very long game to give to her off spring. What a gift for the sacrifices our ancestors make. It was an *unsung hero* moment for her. You won't fully see the outcome. But doesn't it sound like a hell of a mission? To be *the one*. Did you know that almost no one, if anyone at all, will remember you 50 years after you die? Maybe you see this as morbid, maybe you see this as liberating. Maybe this truth will unlock something in you to help you get focused on the goal of attaching yourself to a vision of a bigger life, one that will serve your babies, grand babies, great grand babies, great great grand babies, great great great grandbabies, and so on. A legacy.

In one generation my Aunt and Uncle changed their entire family trajectory. The other two sisters are not doing bad at all either. Aunt Linda did a little land investing based on Aunt Karen's recommendation and has bought and sold several properties, owning her current one free and clear. My parents have their primary home free and clear and have no debt. My sister and I both have rental property portfolios. My brother and his wife are both very successful and both work in real estate. Both of Aunt Karen and Uncle Freddy's adult children own their primary houses and one of them bought some land outside of Austin a couple of years ago and built a tiny home on it as a second home and investment. My cousins from Aunt Gayle are all exceptional, two of which have started early families and went to graduate from Texas Tech. Both of them are homeowners in their early 20s. All four sisters who grew up in a shack in the middle of the woods without plumbing went to university and almost all of us cousins did as well. Home ownership is a primary goal, either achieved or working toward, for almost everyone in our nuclear family. Is this because of Momo starting something here? I truly believe so...yes. And since everyone on earth is born, you came in on the residual of your ancestors who built your starting point. And every single family upline at some point had royalty in it, wealthy family members, government leaders, inventors, truly exceptional people. You just don't know who they are and what happened to their fortunes. But if you just sit with this idea for a moment, isn't it at least plausible that someone before you was a proverbial rock star? Every family tree operates in cycles of abundance and cycles of lack. Elephants realize this. Elephants intuitively understand that it wasn't where they came from, it's where they are going. Once I personally arrived at that inalienable truth, my life was tremendously more peaceful. My narrative shifted from what happened to me, to what happened for me. I was exactly where I was supposed to be made for my own unique calling and purpose.

My Uncle Freddy did not come from those same humble beginnings as Aunt Karen, as his family had started investing in raw land, farms, and real estate, one generation earlier and in an area that would end up booming. His family bought a patch of land in present day Plano, TX about 100 years ago. He is the only pathway in the entire book that came from a wealthier background. My Aunt Karen was for sure first generation. My Uncle Freddy inherited 4 acres of land from his parents as a bachelor. At the core, Uncle Freddy was a rancher. He loved animals, which is why he became a veterinarian and loved working on the land with the animals. I've never known him to not have cattle, donkey's, or miniature horses until a few years ago when he realized he needed to slow down at 80.

Uncle Freddy is one of the kindest people I know, and the most humble multi-millionaire next door I have ever known. He embodied the ultimate role model for me. Humble, kind, quiet, unassuming, *balance sheet* rich before I even knew that was a thing, doing the work he loved, having the hobby of ranching that he loved even more…and financially free. He was my first peephole look into what running a small business looked like. I always had him in my peripheral vision and I would often think 'what would Uncle Freddy do.' He was such a subconscious influence on the type of success I wanted. I know you have a version of Uncle Freddy and Aunt Karen too somewhere in your family tree. Align yourself with the people you want to be like. Jim Rohn articulates this well with his famous quote 'You're The Average Of The Five People You Spend The Most Time With.'

Here is what their portfolio journey looks like, which includes their primary residences (note: because of various buy, hold, sell cycles the list is not perfectly chronological):

Property 1: Their first house. They bought their first house in 1977 in The Colony, Texas two years after they got married. They paid $37,000 and the property doubled in value 7 years later when they sold it for $74,000 in 1983. They did a mortgage on it.

Property 2: Hebron Land and a House. This is the house they lived in to raise their family. We went to that house for Christmas and Easter yearly. The house sat on 3 acres and they bought it in 1983 for $327,000 in Hebron, Texas (next to Plano, TX) The Hebron house was a 3 bedroom, 2 bathroom with a carport and detached 3 car garage. They kept miniature horses on two of the three acres. They sold that house and land in 2006, 23 years later, for $2.1 million to a developer who scrapped the house and built condos. Where did they move with this big jackpot? Would it be surprising that they took their millions and leased a double-wide from a friend for about 3 years, while they decided what their next land buy would be? Millionaire next door Elephants have been known to do things like this. It is not as uncommon as you think. I drive a 2017 Chevrolet Equinox currently with over 120,000 miles on it and lived in an apartment for three years prior to buying my most recent *Move-Up*.

Property 3: Uncle Freddy's Veterinarian building - Once he decided to go into practice for himself, he bought the building to open his Veterinarian clinic in 1986. She can't remember what they paid for it. Isn't that funny? She's a multi-millionaire and can't remember what they paid for a building. But that is how it goes and this does indeed happen when you play the long game. You just can't remember every detail of your investing journey. For most families that have a small business, it is typically a family business and that was exactly their case as well. Aunt Karen would work the front desk and my cousins would work in the clinic doing various things during their summer breaks and other times throughout their lives. Uncle Freddy treated our entire family's pets for their annual exams and would never charge us for his services. He never took one dime from any of our family members for pet services and collectively we had a lot of pets. He was so generous. He never asked for a thank you or kept a mental tally. He was a man of service, giving and very thoughtful. He would go on to sell his clinic in 2015 and the clinic as a real estate asset was a large portion of the business valuation. That is not uncommon actually. According to ExitStrategies.com: 'Owning your real property [real estate] is likely to increase the demand, transferability and selling price of your business. Why? When you control the property, you can offer business buyers more options.'

Aunt Karen doesn't remember how much the building was sold for when they sold it within the sale of the veterinarian practice but the entire price for the practice which included the building was $900,000. So we can't create a direct return on the value of the building. But we know there was a return.

Property 4: Tioga Land with a little apartment built on it. They bought 200 acres in 1993 in the Gunner/Tioga North Texas area. It was a place for Uncle Freddy to work on his ranch and get out of town to decompress from his vet clinic. It was raw land and they never built a house on it (this is why they didn't move there after selling Hebron). They bought this in a fire sale situation. It was being sold for a very cheap cost per acre by the Hunt Brothers as part of the fall out from Silver Thursday. Basically the Hunt brothers cornered the silver market and it backfired, eventually leading them to file bankruptcy. They had to sell many of their assets, this plot of land being one of them.

The Hunt's owned approximately 9,000 acres in Gunner/Tioga and sold them off in 400 acre plots. So Uncle Freddy's brother and him split the purchase both owning 200 acres. They paid $140,000 each which equaled $700 an acre. They got a land loan from a local bank to cover the purchase price which has long since been paid off. Uncle Freddy's brother ended up building a house on his side and selling it in 2000. Uncle Freddy built a little barn and modest apartment type dwelling on his side, but they never lived there. My Uncle and Aunt sold their 200 acres in 2021 for $9 Million!!! That was over a 6000% return. They win the award for the highest return of any other pathway in this book. Why did they get such a large return? Because they 'got lucky' my Aunt Karen acknowledges. Their land was going to be very close to an eventual tollway extension and once that was confirmed, the value increased like Bitcoin's value did. She didn't know that was the case, but did know that land eventually pays off and in the meantime they would use it and enjoy getting a utility value of it just like Momo and Grandpa did on the land they bought.

After this sale, the investment company that bought it has since relisted it for $34 million...and one day they will get it. It's just a matter of which decade.

Property 5: Collinsville Land and Modular Home. Uncle Freddy and Aunt Karen wanted another swath of land that would have more animals like deer and turkey and be deeper in the country than their Gunner/Tioga land. I always found it interesting that both my Uncle Freddy and Aunt Karen clearly longed to go back to the 'living in the woods' mentality they both came from. They purchased land in Collinsville, Texas in 2000. Uncle Freddy was out looking one day with his *SME* and they ran into a random guy who was painting a fence at the gate of another property they were looking at. He said, "What are you looking for? I have another property with deer and turkeys on it. Wanna see it?" They all went and saw it right away and within a week Uncle Freddy made an offer to buy. Aunt Karen hadn't even seen it yet, but trusted Uncle Freddy to lead their decision. While they were renting the doublewide after the Hebron sale from 2006-2009, they decided they wanted to now live on this land and spend their days hearing the whistling of the trees and the gobbles from the turkeys and to nature watch the raccoons and deer who came out at night and were recorded on their land cams. While living in the doublewide, they learned about the process of putting a manufactured house on the land versus building a brick and mortar home from scratch. They decided on the manufactured house pathway. I asked why they didn't want to build a brick and mortar traditional house. She said they were getting older and did not want to deal with all the decisions, or as Aunt Karen puts it, "all the bull sh*t of building a house." They were in the easy street zone of their life. But that was the thing about Aunt Karen, she always made strong decisions that worked for her and her family and stood by them confidently. Not arrogantly, but confidently, which is how Elephants roll. So with a firm decision made, the order was placed for their triple-wide manufactured home. It was made in Austin and delivered and assembled right on their Collinsville land.

It's worth noting that for both their land purchases, the primary reason was for their lifestyle desires, and the investment was the secondary reason. I think in a way that helped them enjoy their investment journey more than only an investor would. If it didn't return as much of a return as it did, it would have mattered less because they were compensated for the enjoyment of using the land over the years. They paid $2500 an acre which totaled $347,500. They borrowed the money again from the same small farming focused bank in Sherman TX that loaned them the money on their Tioga purchase from 1993 and they ended up paying off the loan quickly in 2006 once they sold their Hebron property. This is where they live today and it is currently estimated to be worth 1.5 million.

Property 6: ⅓ of the 88 acres Aunt Karen inherited from Momo and then Grandpa.

What tips would my Aunt Karen give to those looking to pioneer a portfolio in land? She said, 'keep notes on your phone to remember the details and be wise about taxes.' For them, they always have their land zoned agricultural, for the *agricultural tax exemption*, except for a smaller portion around their house. It's a huge savings. Buy something you like, can enjoy, and will hold for a long time. She still believes the *American Dream* is alive and land is a big reason why. If you don't already, will you consider owning your piece of America one day?

TERMS AND THINGS TO CONSIDER FOR THE LAND PATHWAY:

- Raw land- also known as undeveloped land, which is vacant land without existing structures or improvements like roads and utilities
- Improved land- vacant land that already has utilities underground and is ready for building.
- Clearing is the process of removing trees and brush; grading, which levels the land's surface,

- Land Based Due Diligence is the buyer's period to investigate the property; infrastructure, which includes utilities, roads, and water systems and city or county ordinances, environmental reports, etc.
- Agricultural Exemption is a hefty property tax exemption you get in exchange for keeping cattle, hay, other commodities on your land and using it for agricultural purposes.
- Land Loan has much different financing terms than traditional residential financing, unless it has a 1-4 unit residential dwelling on it. Land Loans are more akin to commercial financing terms requiring higher down payments, higher interest rates, and shorter pay back terms compared to a 30-year fixed rate mortgage. Also vacant land is a niche asset for lenders and not all lending institutions offer land loan programs.
- Building Requirements could be required and typically the seller is aware of them. However, you will always need to trust, but verify them for yourself in the Due Diligence period.
- Long Term is the mindset that is needed for land investing. It is simply much less liquid than traditional RPI. Even if you speculate it won't be, Aunt Karent would always advise you to prepare like it will be.

Land is usually an even longer play than traditional RPI, so ask yourself what is your end game? And are you willing to have a strong enough *Willing & Able* mindset to stay on your migration? Just like Aunt Karen reminds, if you are a normal person like she was, it is important to want to use the land and enjoy it and the investment component is secondary.

Here is a look at Aunt Karen & Uncle Freddy's *RPQ*:

Property Name & Details	House #1 - Primary Home	#2 - Land inherited from Uncle Freddy's parents & #3 -Land and House they lived in and raised their family	#4- Veterinary Clinic - Commercial Real Estate	#5- Land with 200 acres and little apartment they sold	#6- Land with 139 acres they live on now with Modular Home	#7- Land Aunt Karen inherited AND #8- Land Aunt Karen bought & gave to Aunt Gayle (full 88 acres)
Year Bought	1977	1977 and 1983	1986	1993	2000	She received in 2019, Momo bought in 1945
Purchase Price	$37,000	$327,000	$60,000	$140,000	$347,500	Inherited in 2017
Down Payment (DP) %	$7,400	$65,400	$12,000	$28,000	$347,500	
Total Cash to Close (DP = Closing Costs (CC)	$7,400	$65,400	$12,000	$28,000	$347,500	
Year Sold	1983	2006	2015	2021		2023
Price Sold	$74,000	$2,100,000	$200,000 - She can't remember the sale price of the building, so I'm using the tax assessed amount from 2015. Entire practice sold for $900,000	$9,000,000		She added in her will to give 58 acres to my Aunt
Rehab Amount	$0	$10,000	0	$100,000*	$200,000*	$0
2025 Value	$342,000	$3,000,000	$330,000	$11,000,000	$1,500,000	$600,000
Total Years Owned	7	19	19	28	25	5

$ Total Equity Gain - Rehab Amount - Ok this is where it is going to get complicated I will use 50% and 25% calculations to show my portion	$37,000	$1,763,000	$140,000	$8,760,000	$952,500	$600,000
% Total Equity Gain	100%	539%	233%	6257%	274%	Infinity % return
% Equity Gain -Annulized	14.29%	28.38%	12.28%	223.47%	10.96%	Infinity % return
ROI (Total Equity / Total Cash to Close	500.00%	2695.72%	1166.67%	31285.71%	274.10%	Infinity % return
ROI (Total Equity / Total Cash to Close -Annualized Return	71.43%	141.88%	61.40%	1117.35%	10.96%	Infinity % return

CHAPTER FIFTEEN

Brian H and Carmen Move-Up pivoting into Mixed Portfolio Pathway

Brian H had a distant view of RPI thanks to his grandfather. In the same way Aunt Karen and Uncle Freddy influenced me in the business, Brian H's grandfather laid the groundwork for him. Before Brian H was born, his Grandpa wanted to leave his engineering job and eventually realized he could with RPI. He decided to buy a few rental properties over time and become a small business owner, owning a small clothing store. This pathway would skip a generation, but would emerge again with grandson Brian H.

Realizing he could buy a property for roughly the same amount he was paying in rent, Brian H decided to make a significant trade-off: buying his first *Move-Up* rental in the suburbs in his 20s when his peers were having their rite-of-passage moment by renting in the vibrant city. Reflecting on his choice, Brian H acknowledged that while he missed out on the city lifestyle with his friends, the trade-off was a necessary step in his RPI migration. Either directly or intuitively he understood the principle of living like a pauper for a little while to live like a king forever. Meaning he did what he 'should' do to get ahead vs doing what he wanted to do earlier than his peers did. This allowed *TVM* to be activated in his 20s which catapulted him ahead in his 40s.

His great migration began in 2005 when purchased his first townhouse in Mesquite. It was a flat market—a market that neither appreciated or depreciated significantly at the time. As a novice investor, he did not fully grasp *economic cycle* dynamics, but his experience highlighted a critical lesson: real estate success often hinges on patience and time. Despite his initial lack of knowledge, Brian H's decision to invest ultimately paid off, reinforcing the idea that real estate tends to work out in the long run. For this particular property, the biggest thorn in his side would turn out to be the HOA. In his words, the property's HOA was a "huge pain in the ass," but he was learning, growing, and was now in the game. These annoying and hard lessons ultimately shaped what his future *Buy Box Criteria* would try to avoid...properties without HOAs.

In 2008, he was ready to buy his second property, closer to the city. Do you see the live like a pauper for a little while to live like a king forever theme starting to bloom? It didn't take him that long to get back to the city and he would return to it with a growing real estate asset.

He bought a second home in Dallas in a popular neighborhood called the M Streets. It was an older home, almost 100 years old but the prices were still very affordable and the area was very sought after because of the proximity to Downtown Dallas. He did a *80/15/5*[10] *loan* in February of 2008 which turned out to be a huge reason for total

10. An 80/15/5 loan means you bought your house with 2 loans and 1 small down payment. The 80% had a primary loan position and first lien position. The 2nd loan of 15% was the secondary loan position. The first loan had a lower interest rate around 6% and the 2nd loan interest rate was around 8%.

global financial collapse, but turned out to be a great lending option for Brian H buying his 2nd property with little money down. In this case Brian H paid $170,500 for the property. His first loan at $136,400 and his second loan at $25,575, totaling $161,975 financed. The down payment he brought to the table was 5% of the purchase price equal to $8,525. Back in the *80/15/5* financing era, there was a lower percent *interest rate* on the larger 1st loan of 80% and a higher percent interest rate on the smaller 2nd loan of 20%. I remember common interest rate combinations back then being 6% on the 1st and 8% on the 2nd.

Those loans do not exist anymore since the *Dodd-Frank Act* brought lending reform after the near fatal *Great Recession* and required changes like *PMI* to be required on every loan with less than a 20% down payment. Additional changes included tightened-up the loan guidelines like the removal of the *Stated Income, Stated Assets (SISA)* loan program which allowed anyone with a pulse to get a mortgage and up to 10 of them. Ever seen the movie *The Big Short*? It was not an exaggeration, that is how it really was from 2004-2008. Unfortunately, we have short memories which is why it is so important to study history. However, over time those safe measures put in place will loosen up—they already are. Be aware of that. History always repeats itself. ALWAYS. Elephants read history and have long memories when few others do. Ever heard the saying, Elephants never forget? Elephants have incredible long-term memories, which are crucial for their survival. Their large, complex brains, with a cerebral cortex more wrinkled than a human's, allow them to recall migration routes, water sources, and even the unique sounds and smells of predators. This "elephant's memory" is most prominent in matriarchs, who use their lifetime of knowledge to guide their herds to food and water during droughts and protect them from danger. Having a long memory, shaped by studying history, helps Elephants not get caught in fear when the headlines try to sell 'the sky is falling' narrative. They can see through the sensationalism and look for the opportunity. There is always opportunity.

The bank barely appraised Brian H's M Streets *SFH Move-Up* because it was nearly unlivable, if that gives you an idea of what a *fixer upper* this thing was. But at that time, if one bank wouldn't have appraised it, then another bank would. And even today, that is still true. Why? Because lenders and appraisers are people. People interpret things differently. Elephants know this. If one lender says no, there is a likely possibility another lender will say yes as long as there is any grey in the situation. Once they closed, Brian H focused solely on getting it liveable. He had a clear goal and he put a lot of *sweat equity*[II] into the *rehab*. This works if you're a talented handyman, but I have seen some awful DIY jobs that added nothing to the value...in fact, a property can be and usually is devalued with shoddy work.

Brian H was just getting in the game, and even though he was still developing his skills, he had a clear *why* and a *SMART*, time-bound goal and he got it done. His free time was spent hauling out trash, sanding floors, updating plumbing, adjusting doors and making it livable for his new wife Carmen. At the time, the City of Dallas was investing in the commercial part of the M Streets called Greenville Ave with funds from the *TIF (Tax Improvement Fund)*. As Trader Joe's went in, walkability increased, and it became a sought after area which he could not have predicted at the time. It was just plain luck... sort of like Aunt Karen and Uncle Freddy's Tioga 6000% return!!! This would also go on to be a winning story for Brian H and Carmen.

After making it livable and moving in a year later in 2010, Brian H then actually tried to sell his Mesquite townhome, but the market was already in a *recession* by this point. He paid $110,000 for it in 2005 and in 2010 it was only worth $80,000 so after it didn't sell and he

II. Sweat equity is value added to the property through the owner's labor rather than financial investment or hiring out the work.

changed his mind in selling it for such a loss, he decided to *pivot* and hold it as a rental. I have seen this as a common starting pathway for some of my RPI, I call it an accidental *Move-Up*. When the property was purchased it was not intended for a rental property, but when the homeowner was ready to move into the next property, the market was in a recession so they just turned it into a rental instead of taking a huge loss. You see, you never really make or lose money when it comes to equity until you *liquidate your asset*. If you want to move and your net equity is underwater, just hold the property as a rental until you are not.

A few years later, they started having children and needed more space and didn't want an older house with more repairs needed. Also there was an opportunity swirling around about a possible promotion for Brian H in Austin. Opting out of buying, they decided to rent as tenants themselves in Richardson for a year until they knew the Austin promotion was on or off the table. Brian was also now under water on his M Streets home as we were in the pit of the *Great Recession* in early 2012, so he had to turn property #2 into a *Move-Up* rental as well. Brian H would be an *Investor-Tenant*, owning two *Move-Up* rentals and being tenants in another landlord's property. That was how I met them. They found me online when I had the property management and leasing division of my first brokerage. I helped them find a property to rent as tenants in Richardson, leased out their M Street house and took over as the leasing and property management of their Mesquite townhome from another *RPI SME* they hired from 2010-2012. Before *Becoming an Elephant*, Brian H was a Fox and we hit it off straight away. He was so laid back and calm. He just 'got it' from the very beginning of his portfolio development.

Remember in the details of my *RPQ*, I outlined that I bought Uncle Bao's rental property condo in 2012, Dee's *Move-Up* rental property in 2015 as well as my first *BRRR* in 2017 from a different client of mine as *pocket listing*? Well I would attempt to do the same with Brian H's M Streets property a year after we initially leased it. He was open to selling it due to the foundation becoming a bigger issue and him not wanting to keep an older home as a rental property long term. I was looking to buy a personal home in 2013 as I wanted to live in the M Street area. He actually wanted to get out of the *RPI Business* in DFW as he was now officially in the Austin area and he felt his money could have a better return there. They actually bought their primary home at the exact perfect sweetheart moment of the recession's trough at the end of 2012 in Austin and saw a great opportunity to buy more. In 2013, the market had started to rebound and his Mesquite property would now break even as opposed to taking a loss and he had a little equity to boot in the M Streets property. I thought about buying both properties from him twice over the course of a decade and I wish I did all 4 times. I honestly wish I had bought every rental property I sold for my clients during the *Great Recession* time frame and actually all the way up to COVID. Everything would have at least doubled in value by now, some properties would have tripled and some would have even quadrupled by 2025.

We didn't come to terms on the Mesquite townhome, but I did put an offer down on the M Street property and he accepted it. We went under contract for $206,340 with me putting $10,317 down. I am including my offer email in its original form so you can see how unconsciously incompetent I was in 2013. Here was the offer email:

From: **Heather A**
Date: Sat, Mar 16, 2013 at 10:25 AM
Subject: M Streets Contract
To: Brian H

HI Brian

Ok here is the contract. I worked up a Net Seller Sheet to show you the net amount you get off 189k you wanted. There are a few seller side closing fees that are nominal and I did not know if you escrow. IF you do then you will not owe the prorated taxes amount at closing...the bank should take care of it. The only closing cost you have is the title policy.

And I rolled up the price by 6% and 6000 in closing costs. IF the appraisal does not get me that purchase price amount, then, I will roll them back out.

Here is the math:

206,340 purchase price

-11,340 Broker commissions

-6000 closing costs

=189,000

The net amount is 185,547 b/c 189,000 - 1411 title - 1742 prorated taxes (if you don't escrow b/c the bank will pay since you already paid) - 150 attorney fees - 50 Currier fees - 100 recording fees = 185,547. There might be a swing in title fees by a couple of hundred, but I just estimated.

The girls (your current tenants) do want to stay and renew in the unit. So what I was thinking was that I could do inspections the first week and once I am out of the option period which is 10 days, then I can give them notice to vacate for 60 days. I could close before their lease is up or at the time it is up to shorten the closing. Whichever you prefer. That way if this deal falls apart because of inspections then you would still have a tenant and the risk is minimal.

Let me know whatever questions you have at all and I will tell you the truth, full honesty, integrity and full disclosure since you don't have representation. If at any point you don't feel good about it, pull the plug. Just want to make sure you are absolutely comfortable since this is my business and not yours, so there is an unfair advantage of knowledge. We have worked together for almost a year now and hope you can trust me, but again, just let me know what I need to do to make you feel comfortable.

I will work on selling your Mesquite home for you next :)

I am sure you noticed the poor grammar and the kindergarten quality of that email. It is best practice to edit your emails before you send them, but I also wanted you to see how deals happen. Remember, this was my real unedited email to Brian H. I actually run companies, have closed well over 1000 transactions, walked over 10,000 houses, built my own RPI portfolio, made millions of dollars from scratch and wrote this book as your *RPI SME* Elephant matriarch...and I wrote an email like that...as a professional. Grammar is not the most important thing. What is the most important thing is that you go after your bright future and claim it because the secret to getting ahead is getting started!

Brian H accepted the offer and we went under contract. I went on to do my inspections and the main beam under the house was bending like a bow and arrow drawn back, which was out of my comfort zone in a big way and so I canceled the contract. I decided I didn't have a lot of experience with 100-year old houses, *pier and beam foundations*, the $75,000 rehab estimate I was about to invest and my time didn't have the bandwidth for this project as I was building my new company by this time. Sometimes it takes going under contract to really analyze your capacity, just like Ben did when he backed out of the *BRRR pivot* he was under contract for. It's ok, if it's not a fit, it's not a fit. My advice is to always follow peace above anything else.

Both of Brian H's properties would go on to double in price within just a few years. I kicked myself over that for years and years. But I eventually forgave myself and said to myself, *if I see a neighborhood that is turning over and sprawling again, I will buy in it.* I would come to make good on that agreement in 2017 with my *BRRR* deal. Nevertheless, Brian H kept it as a rental for many years and we leased and managed it for him. No change in the relationship because as a Fox on his path to *Becoming an Elephant*, there is no blame to be placed on it not working out as we thought.

By 2017 and they had an itch to see how they could scale their *RPI portfolio* which included the 2 rental properties and 1 equity loaded primary residence. After learning of the benefits of a *1031 exchange*, they ran some quick math on learning how many properties they could buy if they did a *1031 exchange* on their M Streets property.

They were interested in doing the exchange for some properties they had identified in a town called Temple, Texas which was about an hour north of Austin. I analyzed the best sell strategy options Brian and Carmen H to meet their *1031 exchange* goals. We thought it best to investigate the *off-market, pocket listing* pathway about potentially selling it to a builder as it was very likely the house was going to be bulldozed and rebuilt from scratch. Builders doing lot scrapes and new construction in the M streets was becoming a trend at that time so the timing was right. I called several builders in the neighborhood that were buying tear downs in the M streets and had them give their *highest and best offer* if they were interested. We sold it for $307,500 cash with a swift 10 day close. They walked away with $187,000 in net profit, after paying fees and the balance of their original 2008 mortgage equal to $99,000.

The *1031 exchange intermediary title company* held their $187,000 net proceeds. Brian H identified 4 properties near Temple and they basically used the $187,000 as the down payment and closing costs on each property, which averaged out to a $46,750 down payment toward each property. The average purchase price of each property was $168,000. They grew their *balance sheet* trajectory by using the same amount of equity to grow their asset value by over 100%. Basically they did have 1 property valued $307,500 gross, and now they have 4 properties valued at $672,000 gross (4 x 168,000).

Now that doesn't paint the full picture as their net worth position has not actually increased by that much because their liability position increased. They only owed $99,000 on 1 property now they owe $550,000 on 4 properties thus making their net worth actually a little less than it would have been without selling because they had fees. Regarding the rental return adjustment, in 2017 they were getting $1700 rent on their dilapidated M streets rental because location, location, location. For their 4 Temple properties they initially collected about $1200 per month per property x 4 which is gross rent income of $5,200. They had HOAs with some of their Temple properties and higher mortgages. But with their M Streets property they had higher repair expenses. I was curious to see how they might have panned out if they just kept their M Streets property and leased it out before it became unlivable, letting the value of the land continue to go up and up. This is the analysis I did for their *RPQ* and you will see the math shortly.

They said Temple was a great area for them because it was near an Army base which allowed renting to army families. Also some families don't want to live on base, adding another reason why rental houses can work really well near military bases. The risk is that the military tenant can be deployed which allows them to break their lease without penalty in the state of Texas. Brian H said that only happened once, and they didn't mind because they left the place in great condition and we were able to quickly and easily re-lease it.

In 2016 Brian H and Carmen bought a property in the M Streets version of San Antonio, TX. By 2018 Carmen got her Texas real estate license and started property managing them herself as their children were more self-sufficient and she had more free time coupled with a deep interest in being more involved in their real estate business just like Yvonne was. One reason Carmen got her license was due to how fast the market was moving. By the time they could make the appointment to see a house with their realtor, it was already sold. It just made sense for her to get her license as they owned 6 houses by 2018 and wanted to grow even more.

Note that Carmen is the only investor turned realtor pathway in this book. It is actually pretty rare but does and can happen for a variety of reasons. It is a pathway you can consider if it matches with your willingness and ability. Of course I have my real estate license, but I was already working in real estate before I became an investor, whereas Carmen's pathway was the other way around.

They sold that San Antonio property a year later and bought 3 others in the Austin outskirts of Georgetown, Round Rock and Tyler, Texas. They found them *off-market* and they all were under $200,000. One was a *FSBO (For Sale By Owner)*, another was a house they had heard about through a *wholesaler*. They had to do some *capital improvements* or *rehab*, and spent about $10,000-15,000 on each property. They went on to sell 3 of these 4 properties in just a few years of ownership because one had an HOA Brian H was triggered by. Another had lots of repairs and they felt like they bought a lemon. They eventually decided to sell the San Antonio property because they didn't want to buy more there and managing Austin, Temple, Tyler and San Antonio was just too much as they re-shifted their focus.

You might be wondering why I seem to be ok with Brian H and Carmen selling some of their properties quickly and I wasn't ok with Leng and Lea doing the same thing. Maybe the difference is because I had worked together with Brian H for years by this time and knew that he and Carmen were super laid back, trusting, big picture, figuring out their pathway foxes. In other words, they were a joy. I knew where they wanted to go with their real estate goals and their *pivots* were understandable to me. I felt like it was iron sharpening iron because my own portfolio had unexpected adjustments, and twists and turns also.

After nine years in Austin, they had been discussing moving to Michigan to be closer to Carmen's family and during the beauty of the COVID's work-from-anywhere era of 2021, they saw an open window and climbed through it. Their home in Austin had appreciated 250% since the 2012 bottom of the *Great Recession* purchase price. The house prices in Michigan were very affordable and they felt they could repeat what they did in Austin. "That was a big deal," he said, adding "we bought close to what felt like a mansion in Michigan for what we originally paid for the Austin house in 2012 which was $300,000." The leftover proceeds from the sale of their Austin home, which sold for $750,000 allowed them to have substantial money in the bank, which was tax free by the way, to prepare for their next real estate investment...yes another *pivot*.

Que increased risk and excitement please. They bought a commercial property that had *mixed-use* renovation possibilities and a *tax incentive*. The building currently had an optometrist's office on the first floor and an unfinished space on the second floor that looked like it was stuck in the 1940s. They contracted an architect and a general contractor and decided to renovate the second floor with four condos. They paid $400,000 for the building (all of the profit from selling their primary home in Austin) and the rehab was approximately $1.2m.

You might be thinking this is a pretty big *pivot*...well sometimes Elephant's get bored of traditional residential RPI. But as an Elephant, you have pathway choices. So they picked another investor pathway and *pivoted* into *mixed-use*.

The main attraction to this property was that it was in an *Opportunity Zone*. Once they finished the $600,000 four condo renovation, they got back $250,000 from the Michigan Community Grant Initiative. There are Opportunity Zone Funds that offer grants like this on the Federal, State, City level. Please take note this is *not* promoted as a new investor strategy and please also note that because it is a government program there are a lot of specific checkmarks that have to be met. In other words, there is risk. These sorts of grants are only given after the work is complete, so much needs to happen before that kickback occurs. There are a number of things that can go wrong that only a seasoned, financially keen Elephant is suited to handle. It doesn't mean this can't be your 101 RPI pathway, but take caution dear friend. There is a reason why babies walk before they run.

Everyone is always curious about how to get 'free' money like these opportunity zones could offer. Here is some more information for how it worked for Brian H and Carmen in the Michigan Area:

MICHIGAN OPPORTUNITY ZONE TERMS:

1. Historic Tax Credits- They can provide for up to a 25% credit for rehabilitating a historic building.
2. Michigan Economic Development Grants- The $250k they got as a rebate of their rehab expenses on their Michigan building.
3. Brownfield Tax Increment Financing- This pays out over 20 years for redeveloping a blighted property (lead paint, asbestos, mold, etc).
4. Neighborhood Enterprise Zone- Freezes property taxes for 12 years. FUN FACT: Our Elephants were actually on the news recently for this improvement they made for the area.
5. Qualified Opportunity Zone Fund- This allowed them to roll the capital gains from the sale of their Texas properties into this project tax free.

Be aware, friend, that there is no free lunch. Brian H says "These incentives are not easy to obtain. It's taken us almost 2 years to line everything up. In retrospect, maybe not the best use of our time or money, but it's been a huge learning experience!" And for Elephants, experiences like this will always be built upon, so they can do it 'better' next time.

Circling back to that Mesquite townhome that started it all, we did indeed finally sell it. But not until the Summer of 2023 for $225,000, which was over twice what he bought it for in 2005. We did a slight rehab on it that took our team a month to do, costing $7,788.

An entire book could be written on Brian H and Carmen. They are a great pathway for the normal person who truly enjoys the game of real estate portfolio building. Like most self-made millionaires say, they might work until they can't anymore, but they don't want to have to if they don't want to.

The truth is, if you buy a stock and the value drops for a year, there isn't much you can do with it but wait. If you buy a house and the value drops temporarily—you can always move back in it. Hold on tight and forge ahead. It won't happen tomorrow or the next day, but it will happen. For Brian H, it took 12 years from his first buy in 2005 to selling in 2017 to reach millionaire status. To date, he and Carmen currently have 6 rentals and the *opportunity zone* fund asset which has the four units and the commercial space. That's 10 residential doors plus 1 commercial asset. They don't know what they will buy next, but they do know they will buy. This is the outlook that active Elephants maintain, *ABL-Always Be Looking*. If this isn't your year to start, maybe it's next year, or the year after. But my hunch is it's probably sooner than you think as long as you are *Willing & Able* because the secret to getting ahead is getting started. This dream is yours for the taking and there is more than enough room for another Elephant at the top.

Here is Brian H and Carmen's 1031 Exchange from Dallas tear down into 4 rentals in Temple near Austin, TX *RPQ*:

2017 GROSS BALANCE SHEET	M Streets Property	4 Temple Properties	
Asset Value	$307,500	$672,000	
Liability	$99,000	$672,000	
Net Worth	$208,500	$0	-$208,500
2025 GROSS BALANCE SHEET	**M Streets Property**	**4 Temple Properties**	
Asset Value	$500,000	$1,200,000	
Liability	$71,000	$594,349	
Net Worth	$429,000	$605,651	$176,651
2017 GROSS INCOME STATEMENT	**M Streets Property**	**4 Temple Properties**	
Monthly Rent	$1,750	$4,800	
Monthly Expenses	$1,125	$4,800	
Gross Monthly Profit	$625	$0	
Gross Annual Profit	$7,500	$0	-$7,500
2025 GROSS INCOME STATEMENT	**M Streets Property**	**4 Temple Properties**	
Monthly Rent	$2,600	$6,733	
Monthly Expenses	$1,750	$5,937	
Gross Monthly Profit	$850	$796	
Gross Annual Profit	$10,200	$9,552	-$648

What are they up to most recently?

In 2025, they purchased another mixed-use property which included a beauty salon and 2 apartments also in Kalimazoo, MI. They bought it for $250,000 and they make $900/mo from the salon and

$1600/mo from both of the apartments which equals $2,500/mo in gross rent. "$250,000 for $2500/mo is the classic *1% rule* which some people say is not possible anymore, but it is if you're patient, buy in the right market timing and market area and are quick to jump on them when they appear", Brian H shared with me. Please note that these successful Elephants didn't achieve this classic rule on any of their other rental properties or buildings until they were already millionaires. If they waited to move until they found a property with the 1% rule, how different would their story have been? I suspect much different because they tapped into the original classic rule of success, which is the secret to getting ahead is getting started. And because they got started, success they have.

CHAPTER SIXTEEN

Trang
HUD houses, Section 8 Pathway

Trang came over from Vietnam a few weeks before Saigon fell in 1975. She was brought over by the US soldier who fell in love with her while on active duty in the Vietnam war. They married and raised a family of 3 children and settled into a life in the United States. She worked as a clerk and cashier at 7-11 as the children grew up. In the late 1990s, the American Red Cross had a program for helping other immigrants migrate to America if they had sponsorship. She was the sponsor for her sisters and brothers to come to America, however one of the conditions was that they needed housing.

The American Red Cross would pay for transitional housing voucher assistance for them to come to America, find jobs and establish a life here. One of her brothers, who was already in the USA, encouraged her to buy houses for their siblings to rent, in which her tenant siblings would pay rent using the housing voucher program. Around the same time, her husband passed away and she received a little life insurance money. She used it to buy her first Dallas, Texas rental property in 1999 and leased it out to one of her siblings and their family. One of the key contacts her brother introduced her to was a Vietnamese *RPI SME* Ann who specialized in helping people do this very thing.

So with this model in place, she bought homes for every relative who was approved to become a US citizen and they used housing vouchers to pay her rent initially until they settled in and found work. It was a win-win. She built a real estate portfolio using *30-year fixed rate mortgages* with very little down payment and the tenants (her family) paid her guaranteed rent through *Section 8 vouchers*[12]. To her, that lowered her risk of collecting rent and allowed her to get started on a mission that would change her entire financial downline for generations to come. Trang was 'the one'.

Many first time investors ask about the Section 8 pathway, here are some synonyms and pros and cons of this pathway I want you to be aware of:

SECTION 8:

Synonyms:

- Section 8
- Housing vouchers
- Housing Department
- HUD (Housing Department of Urban Development)
- Housing Choice Voucher Program (HVC)
- Government subsidized

Keep in mind that public housing vouchers can come from the city, county or federal level. Another common misconception, at least in my market, is that you don't buy a government property, you can buy any rental property and then apply to be a section 8 landlord.

12. Bear in mind, Section 8 vouchers and programs like it require much research and learning. You are working with the government in these cases which can mean slow responses, red tape, and bureaucratic mess.

PROS:

- You get 'guaranteed rent' but there can sometimes be a catch here. See the first con to learn about that
- In my experience the section 8 tenant stays longer than the average 2-year tenant stay, thus reducing vacancy and make-ready expenses
- If you know if this is your pathway, as Trang did, it can be a good thing to be niche focused so you can build deep and not wide
- Sometimes you can get more than the market rent. Sometimes the more bedrooms you have, the more rent you can collect from city and county housing voucher programs.

CONS:

- The housing department will not always pay the entire rent amount. They audit the tenant's case file, typically annually, and if the tenant is making more money than last year they might require them to pay a portion of the rent. For Example, if the rent is $2000, and section 8 pays $1600 on the renewal, you have to collect the additional $400 from the tenant. Sounds easy right? In my experience, that hasn't been the case.
- The response time to rent increase requests can be lengthy because...well, it's the government. I had a rent increase response take almost 4 months one time and no, they would not backdate the increase when they finally approved it
- It can be pretty laborious to get your property initially set up in the system and to be aligned with a tenant that can work for that property. In one of my apartment units, the process took 6 months, the housing department required repairs before the tenant moved-in, and in the end the tenant did not even end up moving in. That was 6 months of lost rent and utility

expenses, as well as the Housing Dept preparation expenses. There was also a mental cost for the months of following up, turning other potential tenants down because we had the unit 'held' and just general annoyance from this situation.

- The Housing Dept will do property walk throughs and require certain HUD required repairs or updates that you normally would not do with traditional tenants.
- Section 8 tenants might not care for your property the same way someone would if they were paying with their own, hard earned money. Remember when you were a kid and your mom or dad yelled at you constantly about turning off the lights when you left the room? Conserving energy wasn't really a value of yours because you weren't paying for it, right? However, as you started paying your own electricity bill, you very well might have turned that light off.

Who says the *American Dream* doesn't exist? Certainly not Trang. She saw an opportunity in a country that gave opportunity to anyone who would take it and she took it! You can take it too! It's available to anyone. Elephants see opportunities others don't. They see whatever everyone else can't always see. I have worked with many first generation Americans and their stories of rags to riches never gets old to me. It is available to every American, but sometimes Americans don't see what they have a birthright to. Freedom! A first world, global leader of a country. Free and mandated education from Kindergarten-12th grade, and bountiful opportunities because of it. Americans can sometimes think the opportunity is outdated and dusty so they may not recognize its inherent value. But first-generation Americans...they can have a childlike curiosity and wonder that drives their success. Boiled down, Trang realized if she takes a little risk, she can help get her brothers and sisters here using America's structure to build the age-old way of building wealth...through real estate.

After Trang's family members got established in America the Section 8 income subsided, which is exactly the way it is supposed to work. According to the *Department of Housing and Urban Development (HUD)* most voucher recipients stay on section 8 vouchers for 6 years, though I personally know tenants who have been on for several decades and even generations, aka *working the system*. Once her family members moved on because they grew in their own *American Dream* real estate endeavors, Trang leased to new tenants she found. She went on to buy and sell property like Brian H & Carmen and myself as well make profit from rent, while building equity. She was also a saver and put as much money as she could in savings, to buy more rental property when the deal was right. Trang is a great example of it's not what you make, it's what you keep and being *balance sheet rich* vs *income statement rich*. She was able to build her rental property portfolio from a single income working as a clerk at 7-11. Yes you heard me right. At her peak of ownership, she had 9 single family rental properties. Today she owns more than half a dozen. She is a multi-millionaire and has amassed this wealth in barely more than a quarter of a century, 26 years.

The main goal she focused on when growing her rental property portfolio was to focus on low vacancy, because she knew low vacancy killed cash flow. She self-managed her rentals, so that was her largest expense. Low vacancy, low vacancy, low vacancy. That was her north star. She started to slash the list price if she went longer than 1-2 months of vacancy...or maybe even sell. She once bought a property that faced Love Field airport in Dallas. She felt the airplane overhead noise was the reason it would not lease out as quickly as her other properties. So after a few tenants and longer vacancies, she decided to sell it. If she held onto it, it would have quadrupled in value today.

It would have been one of her best equity appreciation investments. You live and learn. Elephant investors have strong memories of those hard lessons, but they don't hold grudges against them. If they did, they couldn't move forward. Grudges hold Lone Wolves up a lot, but not Elephants.

Trang was a go-getter and a natural entrepreneur. She invested in a nail salon for a short stint but realized she didn't like working in it and preferred her first love of being a residential RPI so she *pivoted* by selling relatively quickly and went back to buying more rentals by letting her *RPI SME* Ann know to keep on the look out for anything that fit her *Buy Box Criteria*. When Ann would call, Trang would often put option money down on properties she had not even seen—fully trusting in her *RPI SME*, who was also a RPI herself. Are there hard lessons that come from this run-and-gun style? Sure. Lessons in the form of losses, missed expectations, fire drills. But, Trang had Elephant vision.

Does she have any regrets? Yes, selling. Trang wishes she held on to more of her properties. As the years went on she became more savvy on her selling transactions. Many long term RPIs share in her regret—myself included. However, Elephants know how to rebrand their regrets and keep moving forward. They know they must move forward in order to make up for what they "lost" along the way. When you get to Elephant status, you have a soul tie understanding that in the end it will all work out.

For the properties she did hold on to, the areas turned over and *gentrified*, which basically means property values dramatically increase in a sleepy neighborhood/area due to investors buying in the area, usually improving the property and reselling them. If an investor offered her $300,000, she told them she wanted $600,000. Yes, that was typed correctly. Double. She had a gut instinct by this time and knew some of the neighborhoods she was in were more valuable than others. Elephants all have a gut instinct that guides them. That gut can only be built by experience. True experience. Experience means "doing it, doing it, doing it" as Michael E. Gerber would say. The only true pathway to gaining experience is time. There just aren't many hacks to getting experience and remember you have a 99% chance of getting rich slowly and only a 1% chance of getting rich quickly.

Because she didn't have to sell, as Elephants always have choices, she would just wait for years to go by knowing the prices would keep going up. Eventually she would indeed collect her $600,000 on a strategically located *SFH* where developers were buying plots and scrapping houses. Remember, one day the investment firm that bought Aunt Karen and Uncle Freddy's Tioga land will get that $34 million, it's just a function of time.

A quality in Trang that stands out is her single-minded approach to play the RPI game. Her mind is made up: growing the portfolio is the goal. In other words, she is fully *balance sheet*, generational wealth focused. Elephants are not double-minded. Please understand that on the way to *Becoming an Elephant*, most likely all of our Elephants at some time or another danced with double-mindedness. The difference is they didn't stay there. The goal is to Foxify your position as soon as you can on the way to *Becoming an Elephant*.

Did Trang have struggles in the business side of the business? She was a 7-Eleven clerk, first-generation American with English as her second language. So yes, of course, she struggled with things like paperwork, accounting, computer integrations, and so forth. This did not stop her. Pulling on help from her children and others, she eventually built systems and remained a focused woman set on changing her family line. I want to make it clear that it wasn't easy. Everyone in her family made sacrifices for her growing rental property business, which would eventually be their growing rental property business. Is it perfect? No. Is this book perfect? No. Nothing is this side of life. But for normal people like you and me to get ahead financially, you are going to have to build something that has never existed. You will have to take risks and likely do them for a decade or two.

If a widow from Saigon can become a multi-millionaire RPI in a couple of decades, you can too. The glorious *30-year fixed rate mortgage* was a huge hammer she used to build her empire. Did you know the *30-year fixed rate mortgage* backed by the government is completely unique to America and the market is begging for new investors to get in the game and move money and assets around using it to do so. Greg McBride, chief financial analyst for Bankrate said "The *30-year fixed-rate mortgage* is a uniquely American construct." Furthermore, a *30-year fixed-rate mortgage* is unique to the USA because it couples the attributes of being long-term and having a simultaneous fixed-interest rate, when in other countries, it is typically one or the other.

This incredible offer to leverage the majority of debt while you grow wealth is yours for the taking. News Flash: that is how normal people like you and me get ahead. Using debt to build assets and to increase *balance sheet* positions. Trang recognized the offer of debt almost as an inheritance and took it. Elephants claim their inheritance. Will you?

Trang has no plans of slowing down. Just in 2024, she bought a brand new construction investment property in Fate. She is now in her 70s and had been watching the market all year for what to buy in The Dawn of the Golden Age of 2025. Maybe by the time this book is published, she may have a new addition.

Oh and about her *RPI SME* Ann. She passed away a few years ago with close to 50 rental properties. I would say she more than met the goal of success. RIP brave and bold Ann. Thank you for changing the lives of so many. Real Estate does indeed change lives.

This is what Trang's *RPQ* of the properties she still owns looks like:

TRANG HUD HOUSES, SECTION 8 PATHWAY

Property Name & Details	Dallas HUD SFH #1	Dallas SFH #2	Dallas HUD SFH #3	Dallas SFH #4	Dallas SFH #5	Garland SFH #6	Garland SFH #7	Fate SFH #8
Year Bought	2000	2002	2007	2008	2008	2017	2017	2024
Purchase Price	$110,000	$70,000	$120,000	$110,000	$130,000	$230,000	$240,000	$330,000
Down Payment (DP) %	5.00%	5.00%	100%	5.00%	5.00%	100.00%	100.00%	25.00%
Total Cash to Close (DP = Closing Costs (CC)	$5,500	$3,500	$120,000	$5,500	$6,500	$230,000	$240,000	$82,500
Rehab Amount	$35,000	$8,000	$10,000	$0	$0	$0	$0	$0
2025 Value	$500,000	$599,000	$704,000	$460,000	$460,000	$375,000	$380,000	$340,000
Loan Amount	$0.0	$0.0	$0.0	$0.0	$0.0	$0.0	$0.0	$247,500
Total Years Owned	25	23	18	17	17	8	8	1
$ Total Equity Gain - Rehab Amount	$355,000	$521,000	$574,000	$350,000	$330,000	$145,000	$140,000	$10,000
% Total Equity Gain	323%	744%	478%	318%	254%	63%	58%	3%
% Equity Gain - Annulized	12.91%	32.36%	26.57%	18.72%	14.93%	7.88%	7.29%	3.03%
ROI (Total Equity / Total Cash to Close	6454.55%	14885.71%	478.33%	6363.64%	5076.92%	63.04%	58.33%	12.12%
ROI (Total Equity / Total Cash to Close -Annualized Return	258.18%	647.20%	26.57%	374.33%	298.64%	7.88%	7.29%	12.12%
	It was a HUD home so that is why she got such a low down payment	This was a private builder, but it was the same GC and crew of the HUD home builder. One of the guys on the crew, Francisco, is still her maintenance person today. Francisco is in his 70s now.	Sold a house in Centerville a mini mansion and sale of that resulted in her having the cash to buy Delano	Bought both Ansons at the same time.	Paid extra for this one because it had a double garage	She did 1031 exchange into the two garland one	Her brother lives in this one. He lived in the one she sold with the 1031 and relocated him here	She wanted a traditional new construction Rental prop in a new market and did financing to leverage the debt

	2 Rehabs done on it	The land is also valuable on this one. Only if the other neighbors sold, then it might exceed this value.	The land is what makes it so valuable today, They would bulldoze it and rebuild $1 million townhomes	Had section 8 tenants				
	People offer on this one all the time because of the location. So it's hard to value it							
	Had section 8 tenants							

CHAPTER SEVENTEEN

The Catel's Move-Up, 1031 Exchange, 529 Pathway

The Catel's were very savings-focused, like Sonny. They were research driven and goal oriented which helped them make clear, concise, and focused decisions allowing them to move quickly once they made them. I originally met them through the man who I sold my rental property division to in 2014. He had been managing their *Move-Up* rental for a year (which I would eventually help them sell in 2017 and 1031 exchange it into two other newer rentals). Selling my rental property division was my first sale of a business and I learned a lot. I probably left a lot of money on the table, but it's all good because I learned some good lessons about selling businesses and never would have met these kind people if not for that experience.

They liked the area of Frisco, TX and so we focused our efforts there. We looked at very few houses, only taking 1-2 tours, and they made a decision quickly. That would end up being their style for the other transactions we did with them. They were already operating with an Elephant mentality, although at the time I started working with them they were still Foxes. Being decisive and standing by it is very powerful. Decisiveness is the opposite of double-mindedness, which we see in our Goldfish investors. Many of our Goldfish investors simply can't get their rental property business to scale because they can't make a decision. Let me say it again, making a decision is very important. Especially when you build the plan first. The decisions are made in the planning phase. Then when it is time to search you find the property that meets your *Buy Box Criteria* that you and the *RPI SME* made together, then you simply make a decision and *execute*. The only way to get ahead and improve on your craft in life is to take action. Making a decision to *execute* on your plan is taking action. Thinking about it for 12 years means nothing.

I met The Catel's in August 2014 and they closed in September with cash. They were high savers and low risk investors. They were both pharmacists, so they might have made more than your average bear, but it's not what you make, it's what you keep as we learned from Trang's pathway. Don't ever let not having all cash hold you back from investing. Use the bank's money like I did and 90% of our investors in this book and get started if you are *Willing & Able* because the secret to getting ahead is getting started.

Is a high income required to *save big?* It's certainly helpful, but you can ALWAYS save something. Most people spend first and save last, but people who grow money over time save first - even if it is $100 per paycheck - you pay your savings account like you would pay any other expense.

After you pay yourself first, you then pay your fixed expenses second (rent/mortgage, utilities, mobile phone, healthcare insurance, auto expenses, child need or pet need expenses) and then your variable/luxury expenses third (groceries, entertainment, dining out, shopping, travel, new technology, gifts). If you follow this formula, you will always be a saver. Becoming or consistently being a saver is about building a practice. It might be an adjustment for it to become easy, but that's a whole other story. It will take practice and commitment and a long term vision. But. You. Can. Do. It.

The Frisco investment property was their 2nd property to buy as they bought their primary home in 2000. About a decade later they were ready to buy their dream home to raise their children in. They wanted new construction and found a neighborhood that suited them nearby, so they moved into their dream home, and turned their primary into a *Move-Up* rental. Unlike Dee's pathway, the Catel's Fox qualities allowed them to much easier *pivot* into this pathway. They held their *Move-Up* rental until 2017 and things went well for them as new landlords. They thought, ok, we like this type of investment–cash flow, appreciation, opportunity for tax strategy, a safe place for our cash. As this property was approaching its 20th year of age, they were getting a little uncomfortable holding an older property (yes, 20+ years is what we call older in North Texas). Based on their research, risk tolerance and lack of time to do more extensive repairs and updates to their rental, they settled on a principle of wanting to own property less than 20-years-old. They preferred newer construction (5-years-old or newer) as a main focus in their *Buy Box Criteria*. They decided to sell and do a 1031 exchange for 1-2 newer and lower priced rental(s).

When they bought their primary property in 2000, they bought it with a mortgage. They refinanced it in 2002 to get a lower interest rate and as they grew in their savings account, they decided to pay off chunks toward their principal balance of their mortgage in order to pay it off sooner. When I was called to sell their *Move-Up* rental in 2017, the profit would be subject to *long term capital gains tax* and likely would have been at the maximum 23.8% tax rate due to their higher household income. When we were discussing strategy, they were interested in doing a *1031 exchange*[13] with the proceeds of this sale. A *1031 exchange* is offered to any investor wanting to sell their real estate asset and defer their *long term capital gains taxes*, but the rules are very specific and strict. There are no legal loopholes to these rules that I am aware of currently.

IRS 1031 EXCHANGE RULES:

1. A 1031 exchange is only usable on certain investments. Here is the description of the 'what can be exchanged': Both the relinquished property you sell and the replacement property you buy must meet certain requirements. Both properties must be held for use in a trade or business or for investment. Property used primarily for personal use, like a primary residence or a second home or vacation home, does not qualify for like-kind exchange treatment. Both properties must be similar enough to qualify as "like-kind." Like-kind property is property of the same nature, character or class. Quality or grade does not matter. Most real estate will be like-kind to other real estate. For example, real property that is improved with a residential rental house is like-kind to vacant land. One exception for real estate is that property within the United States is not like-kind to property outside of the United States. Also, improvements that are conveyed without land are not of like kind to land. Real property and personal property can both qualify as exchange properties under Section 1031; but real property can never be like-kind to personal property. In personal property exchanges, the rules pertaining to what qualifies as like-kind are more restrictive than the rules

13. A 1031 exchange, named after Section 1031 of the Internal Revenue Code, allows investors to defer paying capital gains taxes on an investment property when it is sold, as long as another like-kind property is purchased with the profit gained.

pertaining to real property. As an example, cars are not like-kind to trucks. Finally, certain types of property are specifically excluded from Section 1031 treatment.

2. Section 1031 does not apply to exchanges of:
    a. Inventory or stock in trade
    b. Stocks, bonds, or notes
    c. Other securities or debt
    d. Partnership interests
    e. Certificates of trust
3. You will work with an intermediary that will work with the title company. NOTE: Please work with a title company that understands how to do 1031 exchanges.
4. The intermediary will hold your sale proceeds in escrow, meaning you don't get the proceeds in your bank account. If you did, that would be called a sale, but with a 1031 exchange, you are not selling, you are exchanging. Thus avoiding a taxable event. Eventually you will likely pay taxes when the property you are buying is sold without using a 1031 exchange, but I have heard stories of the generational rich that only use 1031 exchanges and use cash-out refinances, which are tax free, to pull equity from the property, but continually defer the property sale. It's really nifty stuff and the stuff you get access to when you take the business behind the RPI Business seriously and run after all that it can offer.
5. The IRS has strict rules as to when you must identify the property you are going to exchange to. The exchange rule states you can designate up to three potential properties within 45 days of closing on the property you are selling and you must close on at least one of them you designate. You might be able to designate more than three if they fall within certain valuation tests.

6. You must close on one of the designated properties within 180 days of closing on the property you are exchanging.
7. If you don't end up identifying in 45 days and closing in 180 days, or you change your mind and just want to 'cash-out.' You can. At that point the intermediary will place your proceeds in your account and it will revert back to being a traditional sale.

Don't let reading about this advanced tool scare you. This tool is in the tool belt of every single wealthy American, I assure you, and has been since it was created in 1921. You just need to be aware of the 1031 exchange and have it in your tool belt. It doesn't mean you will be ready to use this tool just yet, however. If you only remember the name of it, that is good enough for now. You can't even consider using this tool until you build equity anyway.

When I was running the numbers for the Catel's *1031 exchange*, I suggested with a little more cash from their savings coupled with the net proceeds from the exchange, they could have two more rentals. This idea really clicked for them because they thought this could be their version of the 529 plan[14] for their two kids. One house each. They could hold each of these houses for 10-15 years in order to pay for their college educations.

This is not the first time I had heard of this 529 Plan substitution. Sometimes people just don't want all their investments in the stock market. They value and invest in the 401k, IRA, Roth IRA, 529 Plan, personal custodial account (i.e. Vanguard, Fidelity, etc). Even crypto currency investing is stock market 2.0 investing and yet another digital asset. But they like tangible, tried and true investments like rental property. Rental properties make forced savings accounts because it

14. The 529 plan is an IRS approved account in which proceeds used toward college are not taxed.

takes an incredible amount of steps and potential up-front money to do the make ready to actually sell one. It is not the next day or same day like a stock trade is. It's a lot harder and requires more thought to liquidate a rental property. This offers you a very good vehicle to force you to save for your future self and generational downline as well as providing a set it and forget it plan.

Investor fatigue is a real thing. I am a savvy investor and I understand finance, and yet it still confuses me when I have to make quarterly and annual decisions about what to invest in, where to invest, what to buy, what to sell. Many Elephants and even some Foxes like simplicity, like a set it and forget it mentality. Meaning they buy the property and don't even consider selling it for at least a decade, usually more...no matter what happens. It's a muscle and most first generation millionaires will have to build it to reach their goal. I know I did, and honestly am still learning and especially as I dive into different investment verticals.

We did a paint, flooring and foundation make ready at the property they exchanged and closed it in December 2017. Because we had to act quickly, due to the 1031 exchange timeline, we started the search on the two they were to buy. They purchased two houses within a week of each other and we closed in February of 2018. They were focused on meeting the timeline requirements of the *1031 exchange* vs every detail of the property needing to be perfect. Elephants know that *done* and *good enough* is always better than *perfect.* That is the attitude you must have when doing an exchange, especially a sell 1, buy 2 exchange. Let me tell you friend, there are a lot of moving parts for everyday investors like us. Jobs, kids, school, work, travel. Executing your investing plan without doing a 1031 exchange has an incredible amount of roles and responsibilities, so adding the pressure of strict timelines, budget goals, and available inventory, micro and macro market conditions plus them doing their normal life is quite an undertaking. Of course it all worked out well and their investments are doing well.

Here are the details of their 1031 exchange.

- New Construction turned *Move-Up* Prop #1 - 5/4/2 *SFH* built in 2000 with 3293 Sq Ft - This was their first home they bought in 2000 as their primary residence. They then built their 2nd primary residence, more like their Dream home, and turned property #1 into a rental property in 2013. It started needing larger repairs as it was getting older and they decided they wanted to sell it and buy newer property. We decided to do a *1031 exchange* into two properties. To sell this house, my brokerage led a small renovation of paint, flooring, foundation repair and a punch list for about $12,000. Since their loan was paid off they decided to exchange the entire proceeds from the sale minus realtor commissions, title fees, and negotiated repairs which equaled $340,576. They took this amount plus another $138,424 from their savings to exchange into the two Fate properties.
- Fate Property 1 Acquisition: It was purchased for $229,00 and leased at $1,850. Currently worth $308,500 in 2025 and leasing at $2,395.
- Fate Property 2 Acquisition: (same city, different neighborhood). This was purchased for $250,000 and originally leased at $1,895. Currently worth $328,000 in 2025 and leasing at $2,495.

The Catel's are Elephants because even though they paid cash for all of their rentals, their portfolio is worth more than $1 million. Here is their *RPQ*:

Property Name & Details	Prop #1 - New Construction turned Move-Up - 5/4/2 SFH built in 2000 with 3100 Sq Ft.	Frisco #2 - 5/3/2 SFH built in 2006 with 2950 Sq Ft	Fate Prop #3 - Bought using 1031 Exchange proceeds from Prop 1- 3/2/2 SFH built in 2012 with 1650 Sq Ft	Fate Prop #4 - Bought using 1031 Exchange proceeds from Prop 1 - 4/2/2 SFH built in 2015 with 2000 Sq Ft	TOTALS (Not including Prop 1 b/c of 1031 Exchange
Year Bought	Oct 2000	Sept 2014	Feb 2018	Feb 2018	
Purchase Price	$220,000	$222,500	$229,000	$250,000	$701,500
Down Payment (DP) %	10%	100%	100%	100%	
Total Cash to Close (DP = Closing Costs (CC)	$27,000	$228,500	$235,000	$256,000	$719,500 (props 2-4)
2025 Value or Sale Value	$370,500	$478,800	$308,500	$328,000	$1,115,300 - (props 2-4)
Total Years Owned	17.25 (1031 exchanged 10-2017)	11	7.5	7.5	
$ Total Equity Gain	$150,500	$256,300	$79,500	$78,000	$413,800
% Total Equity Gain	68%	115%	35%	31%	181%
% Equity Gain - Annulized	3.97%	10.47%	4.63%	4.16%	19.26%
ROI (Total Equity / Total Cash to Close	557.41%	112.17%	33.83%	30.47%	176.46%
ROI (Total Equity / Total Cash to Close -Annualized Return	32.31%	10.20%	4.51%	4.06%	18.77%

The question I had is would they have made the same returns if they instead took their $479,000 investment (their Prop #3 at $250,000 and Prop #4 at $229,00 = $479,000) and put it into a 529 plan? Probably. They would not have had access to the extremely valuable business side of RPI including Pillar #1 LLC set up and Pillar #2 tax strategy to offset their personal income tax and net cash flow they received from their rental properties, but their 529 plan would have returned yield for sure.

Honestly, either way would have probably been ok. That is why it is important to qualify yourself so you can discern your investment vehicle and then get started. Because the Catel's chose real estate, they were given far more *choices.*

For example, if they decided they didn't want to sell their rental property and still pay for their children's college, they could:

1. Do a *cash-out refinance* up to 80% of the property's current value (in Texas anyway). Since they already paid cash, it is free and clear, but even if they didn't pay cash, in 10-15 years when their kids would be ready for college, they would have enough equity and enough mortgage paydown by the tenant to take out a significant amount of equity. This *cash-out refinance* is tax free. It's a super cool tool you use to keep the rental property asset while it continues to grow in value and you use it like your own bank.
2. If you did take loans on the property and the interest is higher, you could take chunks of money and apply it toward a principal recast and increase your cash flow position thus allowing you to take that cash flow and pay for their school monthly.
3. If the properties were free and clear you might have enough money per month collected in net rent to pay for their school each month with cash flow.

All three of these options allow you to keep the property, still using tax strategy opportunities as well as letting the property appreciate in value.

Their children did start University recently and they ended up choosing to not sell their 529 plan properties, but the point is they were prepared and had the plan in place should they have needed to. Owning rental property is all about having choices. Planning ahead gives you those choices, glorious choices.

CHAPTER EIGHTEEN

Brian L Mobile Home Parks Pathway

I met a Fox turned Elephant named Brian L back in 2017. He worked for a tech company, but was about to take the leap out of corporate to become a full time real estate investor. He was referred to me through the same group that Tom the Lone Wolf got me kicked out of. Before I met him he was already a RPI, as Brian L and his wife bought their first rental when he was turning 30 back in 2011 in CA. It was a condo in Fremont, CA. A little later that same year, they bought a townhome in a different suburb of San Francisco to move into, thus turning their Freemont condo into their first *Move-Up* rental. However, they stayed only a year in their townhome because they realized the commute was too long, so they turned it into another *Move-Up* rental property, had their tenant move out of the Freemont Condo and moved back into it until 2016, when his wife got a job offer in New York City. They turned the Freemont condo back into a *Move-Up* rental...again and now they had two *Move-Up* rentals and they themselves became tenants renting an apartment in NYC, never buying anything. They lived in NYC from 2016-2018 and as Brian L continued to get the real estate bug, he thought about how he could diversify and be a full time investor.

As timing would be on cue, his wife got a promotion at a tech company that would move them back to San Francisco. He decided to make his move and start his real estate investing career. Before he left his W2 job, however, he wanted to go ahead and get another rental property while he could qualify for a traditional investment property loan as a W2 employee, the easiest way to get qualified for a *30-year fixed mortgage*. They decided to try their hand at a DFW Texas rental. We found him an investment property pretty quickly in Plano, Texas. He was a seasoned Fox and had such a calm, trusting, laid back demeanor. He was a joy to work with. He made a big impression on me. I have heard that people remember kindness above anything else. I have never forgotten Brian L's kindness.

You might be thinking, why would Brian L leave a stable career like he had to pursue something so risky? Elephants in the making, like Brian L, are clear that everything has some level of risk. Brian L wanted to think big, and what he was about to pursue was definitely big.

He signed up and paid $10,000 to a Mobile Home Park Coaching Bootcamp one weekend in January of 2016 and this business model excited him. After that, he and his investing partner bought their first mobile home park in Dayton, Ohio just a few months later. They paid $275,000 for it and paid cash. It was 55 spaces with 30 of the spaces leased out. It was pretty distressed. The mobile homes were anchored to the ground and as the owner of the park, he owned the land and was responsible for providing sewer, water, gas lines, utility line hookups, trash services, upholding the community guidelines and up-keeping the concrete pads the mobile homes sat on.

So basically, he owned the land plots which included utility connections and he offered property management responsibilities to the tenants that leased the mobile home spaces from him. He collected rent on the land he rented to the mobile home tenants who used his land and utility hookups for their mobile home. The main difference in this model than most of the pathways you have heard so far, is that Brian L did not own the homes. The tenants owned their mobile homes and were renting the land. He focused his geographical area on the midwest of the USA as this made sense for his price range and size of park he could manage. He said it took a few years to stabilize his first park as he was given the 'adventure' of removing drug dealers, dealing with a fire, evicting 17 of the 30 tenants, rehabbing the property abandoned by some of those evicted tenants, being a victim of General Contractor fraud, and so forth. Does this sound fun yet to you? Because Brian L sees things as an Elephant, he saw this as a lesson in the pathway he was committed to rather than a deal breaker situation.

Brian L taught me about patience when I worked with him in 2017 and again while interviewing him for this book so many years later. He has the 'it' factor for being a guy that can stay the course, not lose his cool, find self-starting motivation and keep his eye focused on the result. He says yes, and doesn't waiver. He reminds me of Michael Jordan when he said, "Once I made a decision, I never thought about it again." Elephants maintain a simple optimism rooted in process and are great at standing by their decisions, no matter what. When you stand by your decision, no matter what, you are not rooted in double-mindedness like a Goldfish. To be successful, you must move forward and standing by your decisions allows you to do that. Additionally, with a consistent process, a successful outcome eventually shows up. What do you think you are buying with McDonald's after all? You are buying a process, aren't you? You can get the same quality anywhere in the world, right? When you see those golden arches in any airport abroad, or off any autobahn in Europe, or in a desert in Dubai, you receive what you expect to receive. You are not buying a hamburger, you are buying a process. Beyond a McDonald's building and land value, their process is their second most valuable asset with franchisees paying well over $1 million for it. So, Brian L kept focusing on his mobile park business process of buy, stabilize, increase value, and sell. And that is exactly what happened.

I don't even know how to make a *RPQ* for Brian L's exciting migration, so here is the narrative overview:

- Condo in Fremont - Lived in it then turned it into a *Move-Up* rental.
- Townhome in a suburb north of San Francisco - Lived in it and turned it into a *Move-Up* rental and moved back into the Fremont condo. From there they moved to NYC for his wife's job relocation and they rented there for a couple of years.
- 2016 mobile home park buy #1 - Ohio
- In 2017 he bought a *SFH* rental with us in Plano, TX. He paid $240,000 with 25% down. He was referred to us with value and wanted smooth sailing in the transaction. We closed in a couple of months and it was a very easy deal on all ends.
- 2017: He bought two more mobile home parks.
    - Indiana: He paid $390,000 for 50 spaces and got a commercial bank loan from a local bank in Indiana.
    - Kentucky: He paid $1,800,000 for 135 spaces. He got seller financing on this, which is the only way he could have done it as he would not be approved by traditional commercial bank financing.
- 2019: He stabilized Kentucky, made some improvements and got it turned around and the majority of the lots leased out and did a *1031 exchange* on it to buy two more.
    - 2019: *1031 exchanged* Kentucky for $4.6 Million to buy a Kansas park for $1 million which had 100 spaces and 70 current tenants.
    - 2020 (right before COVID): Used the remaining proceeds from Kentucky to exchange into St. Louis for $3 million.

It had 188 spaces and 70 occupied tenants. He describes with laughter "that Kentucky was the nightmare of his life". He said it took a tremendous amount of energy to run this business model, which was to buy manufactured houses, add them to the lots, market them, sell them, and close them. He was essentially acting as a builder in a new construction community and doing it virtually from CA where he lives, rather than in the local market.

- 2019: Sold Indiana mobile home park for $700,000 as they just didn't like it. He didn't do a *1031 exchange* on it and just paid the *long term capital gains taxes* and moved on with his Elephant life. Sometimes, you just pay the taxes and move on. When Aunt Karen sold their land in 2021, she said she wrote a $2 million check to the IRS. It happens.
- 2020: He sold Dayton, Ohio for $1 million and also didn't do a *1031 exchange*. He said they also just didn't really like the Ohio location and also got a little nervous about COVID as they didn't know what the market would do. Join the club right? This is universal, whether you are an Elephant, a pundit, or a fortune teller: the markets cannot be perfectly predicted by anyone.
- 2021: We sold his Plano house for $320,000. He did not do a *1031 exchange* on it. It is worth around $375,000 as of 2025. When we spoke for our interview, he said he regretted selling it and should have held it. I reminded him there are no regrets, only lessons. He reminded me why he loved working with us. I reminded him how much I appreciated working with him.
- 2022: He bought a second St Louis mobile home park located just a few minutes away from his other St Louis mobile home park. They just really liked the St Louis area. He said it is tremendously valuable to have two Mobile Home Parks within 15 minutes of each other. That will be an incredible addition when

> they sell them in approximately 5 years. Also they already have a vendor pool in the area which was a tremendous value in on-boarding their new asset because the vendors they have for park 1 can work on park 2 when needed. He said they paid a bit of a premium but they had their reasons, mainly described above. They invested $6.4 Million for 138 spaces.

There are only about 45,000 mobile home parks in the USA, whereas there are about 82 million single family homes. Why would Brian L go into this business when there is only .05% of the supply of single family homes? First of all, there are not that many people wanting to buy mobile home parks. The reason is that to buy a mobile home park you need to be well capitalized and prove you have the capacity and experience to close on a commercial loan. With *commercial loans*, the main differences are the *amortization* period is generally 15-20 years (compared to 30 years) and the interest rate is usually only locked in for 5-7 years compared to *30-year fixed rate mortgage*. It's a different and more risky game that requires a more capitalized and experienced investor.

Beyond that, mobile home parks that don't have mobile homes affixed to the earth are not considered real estate assets that appreciate. They actually depreciate like a car would. They are considered motor vehicles and are not a home at all, but a big car that you can live in. Some banks won't finance them because they are not attached to the earth. It's just a business that most people can't relate to, understand, or honestly desire to be in. Also because there are so few mobile home parks in the USA, you will likely acquire them in many different states which can create long-distance logistics.

So is Brian L a crazy, wild man investor? Maybe, according to some. But to me, he is a hero. He is an Elephant who focused on specializing in this niche space allowing him to build deep and not wide, scale quickly and amass a stunningly hefty *balance sheet* with acreages of land leveraged by other people's money. With this business model, there was for sure a learning curve for Brian L, but he knew there would be. He had the time, treasure and talent to focus on it and play the long game. To date he has 3 mobile home parks remaining with 426 spaces in 2 different states worth well over $10,000,000 in property value. Not bad for a normal guy just like you and me from Pennsylvania born to first generation immigrant parents.

I asked him if he thinks the younger versions of himself could do this today. He replied, "Prices have indeed changed. Essentially we bought the same property in Kentucky for $1.6 million in 2017 as we did in St Louis for $6.8 million in 2022. It is simply more expensive, but that doesn't mean it isn't doable." Perhaps a niche investor in 2025 would need to consider other real estate asset types. Maybe it's storage facilities, or car washes, or raw land, or micro houses or syndicated real estate investing, or crypto real estate investing, or buying duplexes in B or C markets and living on one side and renting out the other. Regardless, at any stage in every season, there is opportunity to be claimed if you are *Willing & Able.*

Let's look at the differences in some of these different types of properties discussed above:

PROPERTY TYPE DETAILS:

Property Type	Micro Home	Tiny Home	Mobile Home	Modular / Manufactured Home	Single Family Home (SFH)
Attached to the Land?	Yes	Yes if attached to a foundation	Yes if attached to a foundation	Yes if attached to a foundation	Yes
Appreciating or Depreciating?	Appreciating	Depreciates like a car	If mobile, it will depreciate like a car	More likely to depreciate	Appreciating
Residential financing?	Yes	Possibly	Possibly	Possibly	Yes

What are the local market opportunities for you? What pathway is right for you right now? What is available? What is the next generation plan for the aging out shopping malls? What can be done with raw land in the short term and the long term to get the agriculture exemption? What seller financing opportunities exist if you can't get traditional financing? Think about what your town or surrounding town can offer like Brian H and Carmen did in Michigan. I promise you there is at least something if you will lean in, self-educate, and act and agree to playing the long game.

For Brian L, he attended the Mobile Home Boot Camp to help him create his Mobile Home *Buy Box Criteria* and *RPI Business* plan, which he said was the only formal and paid training he ever invested in by the way. That is exactly what Elephants do. They get educated, but then they do the next most important thing...they *execute.* Because....everybody in unison now...if you are *Willing & Able*, the secret to getting ahead is getting started.

CHAPTER NINETEEN

Pick your Pathway if you are Willing & Able and Execute

The main goal of this book is to help you qualify yourself for your *ability* and *willingness*, articulate your *why*, and learn about pathway case studies from normal people just like you and me so you can *Pick Your Pathway* and *execute*. I hope it is clear by now that the secret to getting ahead is getting started if you are *Willing & Able*. The book was designed to categorize different investor personalities, so you can help identify who you are, who you might have been and who you want to be. This book hopefully provided a clear action plan and a glimpse into your potential future as a RPI, using real examples of ordinary people on their way to *becoming*, or who have *become*. If RPI isn't for you, this book encourages you to rule it out for now, or forever, and move closer to finding your ideal investment strategy. Your dream life is attainable. To be a millionaire you just need roughly 4-rental properties and about a generation to change the financial trajectory of your family lineage for generations to come. You can use the *4-in-10,* which is to acquire 4 properties within 10 years and then pay them off from years 11-20 using the *debt snowball method*. You can use the *4-in-10* and overlay it with any of the pathways you have read about to give you a clear process, systematic planned approach like Yvonne and Mike did. Or you can use your own marriage of any of these pathways that spark your fancy. All that you really need to commit to for step 1 is if you are *Willing & Able*, then *Pick Your Pathway* and get started because the secret to getting ahead is getting started.

Another key lesson here is don't focus too much on the get rich quick plans that yield a 1% chance and forgo the get rich slow plans which yield a 99% chance of success. The reality is that you can build wealth in just one generation. The formula is simple, but I didn't say it was fully easy. It indeed takes commitment, skill, adjustment, agility and perseverance. That is why even in America, and even in the 21st century with the age of unlimited information and AI, it is still hard for most to be a millionaire and for most to live below their means. To get rich slowly in one generation is very likely for most, but most won't do it and continue to look for get rich quick routes, missing the get rich slow train.

Consider your choices, friend. Pull out a pen and set a schedule. At some point Ben had to become Ben, Trang had to become Trang, Heather had to become Heather and now you have to become you. Like all of us in this book, we weren't and then we were. It's a series of *moments*. You had a *reason* that you invested in this book. You recognized that it was an investment and not an expense. Absorb these pathway case studies, pack one in your heart and believe it can be true for you too. One day...I may be writing about *you*.

LET'S RECAP OUR ANIMAL PERSONALITY TRAITS:

Fox: They are the scrappy ones, just starting out, maybe skittish, a little timid, unsure, but once they figure it out they dominate. They outsmart dogs and chickens, they survive. They are less emotional because they are more relational and value the people they hired to lead. They are usually managers or they work on teams. Foxes know there is a long race ahead, about 20 years or so, and are good with that, but sometimes just don't know how to get started. They have run a few races before in business, investments and life, which is how they learn to sit back and play the long game in order to win the race. The Fox could easily set themselves up to be an Elephant if they increased their risk tolerance a little bit more. If we increase one variable in the race, like speed, distance, velocity, altitude, we can adjust the pace. You usually stay at your W2 job as a Fox and receive income from that. You save it at a higher pace because you're driven to save more down payments to buy investment properties. Foxes desire to pursue having 3-4 rentals under their belt. Foxes learn to wait and be patient and let the time value of money do its thing. Foxes have an innate understanding that everything is just going to work out. And you know what, it does

Lone Wolf: They are the DIY type, prone to being controlling and don't play by the leader's rules. They generally don't value *RPI SMEs* they hire, but somehow still need one to do the deal. They have other people do their bidding but they still try to be the alpha. This results in them being the hardest to work with, and they come with the most growing pains because they don't take the advice from those who have done it. Most Lone Wolves don't want to be alone, they want to be with their pack—they just don't know how. Lone Wolves could find their way into being an Elephant financially, but it is unlikely, because they don't delegate and people usually don't want to work with them. This stifles their ability to scale. To a Lone Wolf, nothing is relational and everything is transactional. They ask your opinion, but only to validate their own opinion, as opposed to learning and growing in community

Goldfish: You tell the Goldfish what to do, they will be agreeable with you, but then it's like they forget or change their mind shortly after.

They are typically very loyal. They are laser focused on their goal even though the market timing and reality of their goal might not be in the present. The leader has to be very bold with the plan for the Goldfish and then they will follow, but not right away. They need to test out their own plan first. Goldfish are loyal, yes, but because their goals are so niche and finite and specific—most people won't work with them. It usually does take much longer because they won't adjust easily. They are slow thrusters who sometimes struggle to articulate their vision. They swim around their tank, without getting anywhere.

Elephant: They are almost always self-made millionaires and see money as a game.

Inherently they know it's a long game and they are willing to play it. They are humble. They are financially free. Usually frugal, but not cheap. They outsource and believe in building teams...good teams. They will work with their team to improve in areas their team needs to grow in. They delegate to their team and trust them to carry it out. They trust, but verify the work. They are the risk takers—maybe it is innate, maybe it is built. They are rarely emotional and when they are, they clean it up because they value people and have a lot of experience working with teams. They are usually generous with their time or helping other people develop by mentoring them or sharing industry knowledge. They are kind and care about people, but they are not pushovers. They are role models and usually the people you aspire to be. Confident, not arrogant. They see their life as it's not where they came from, it's where they are going.

Overwhelmed?

I would be surprised if you weren't. These *Pick Your Pathway* case studies and lessons were taken from real RPIs that were normal people like you and like me. How could you drink that in one gulp? I think the only way is if you were some real estate investing savant and honestly if that was the case you would not have needed to read this book anyway. For most of us it is about getting started or buying the next property if you are *Willing & Able*.

The goal of me laying out all of these investor pathways is so you can fill in the mysterious 'how' component and see the truth about normal people like you and me do this. Remember, there's no way you could know what you don't know so you really need to keep it simple and put your little blinders on like a horse in a race and stay focused on your track. I highly recommend working with a *RPI SME*. All Elephant's outsource, we hire other people that are better at doing what we want to do so we can focus on our skills and have less pain and more enjoyment out of it. Plus if I spend my time focusing on my talent, then I will make way more money and develop greater opportunities than I would going to learn how to do it myself like a Lone Wolf does.

Either way you're gonna pay for it. Trust me...do it with the right people, whatever that means to you. To me, it means to build a really great team if I'm going to go buy a rental property. If I'm going to train for an Iron Man competition, then I'm going to need a really great Iron Man coach that understands bicycling, swimming and long distance running, wouldn't you agree? This is no different. Running in an Iron Man is an elite and specialized dedication that not many people truly get or understand. Successful RPI is similar.

It's kind of absurd to even consider doing something like this on your own. And no, the internet is not a replacement for real world relationships and neither is Chat GPT. Newsflash: the internet can actually make things more complicated in many cases, especially when something is already complicated. Want to set up your smart home, go ahead and YouTube it. Let me know how easy that was for you. The internet and AI are excellent, valuable tools, but they have a place. Remember at the core this is a market-specific and people business. Every house, piece of land, market climate on a micro and macro level, ability to get financing, property type, tenant class, *RPI Business* plan is all specific and unique to YOU and your goals. It's really hard to find answers to people's unique situations solely on the internet. It's a tool in the same way a hammer is, use it as such.

All I ask is whatever you do or don't do you see it as a lesson, and always move forward. Make that promise now, dear friend. You won't believe how much your psychology will be an active participant in this investing vertical. You are never a failure, just a constant work in progress. If you choose that perspective, you cannot lose because you cannot lose unless you give up and you're not going to be giving up because you have great work to do, my mighty friend. You have beautiful, life-giving, generation building, memory-making, meaningful, big work to do. You're going to change the financial trajectory of your downline for generations to come. You can make that agreement now if you wish. Decide that is the gift you'll be leaving behind.

Don't let anyone tell you any different, as misery loves company and people like to bring you down if they are down. Fly with the eagles, don't walk with the turkeys. Discern. Only take advice from those in this specific niche vertical who can lift you up and help you learn how to do what you desire, not that you can't do it. Never go to the hardware store to buy bread and if your extended family doesn't get it, don't discuss it with them. Make this important boundary. It will save your dream. As I type this very sentence, a non-aligned acquaintance called and asked me what I was doing. I said, "Organizing some information" and moved on. But when my book publisher calls me next Thursday, I will speak to him quite differently about what I am doing. In other words, protect yourself against anyone who isn't in full alignment with your *why*. And I mean anyone. There are a lot of dream killers out there and you will have to protect yourself. You are actually the only one who can.

As I close I want to bring in our matriarch and patriarch quote gurus one last time. In the words of Mary Oliver, "Tell me, what is it you plan to do with your one wild and precious life?" And in the words of Mark Twain "the secret to getting ahead is getting started." With that, if you are *Willing & Able*, *Pick Your Pathway* and read Mark Twain's quote again.

Thank you for trusting me to be your *Becoming the Elephant* matriarch. Now go thrive my friend.

Heather Lynn Anderson has been in the rental property investing world since 2003—long enough to have seen the highs, the lows, and everything in between (including a few "what was I thinking?" moments). She's built her own rental property portfolio from the ground up and has helped hundreds of investors do the same—without losing their sanity or their sense of humor.

Heather is passionate about helping people just like you get started—if rental property investing actually makes sense for your life (because not every deal—or dream—is created equal).

When she's not talking tax strategy and contracts, you'll find her diving into quantum physics (yes, really), traveling God's beautiful earth, and encouraging the incredible people she meets along the way. She's deeply grateful for this wild ride of a life—and all the blessings that pour of it.

For more information or to follow up online,
visit or scan the QR code below:

www.RentalPropertyU.com

www.ingramcontent.com/pod-product-compliance
Lightning Source LLC
Chambersburg PA
CBHW031341230926
51848CB00002B/337
9781967262410